Grandma Doralee Patinkin's Jewish Family Cookbook

ST. MARTIN'S GRIFFIN

NEW YORK

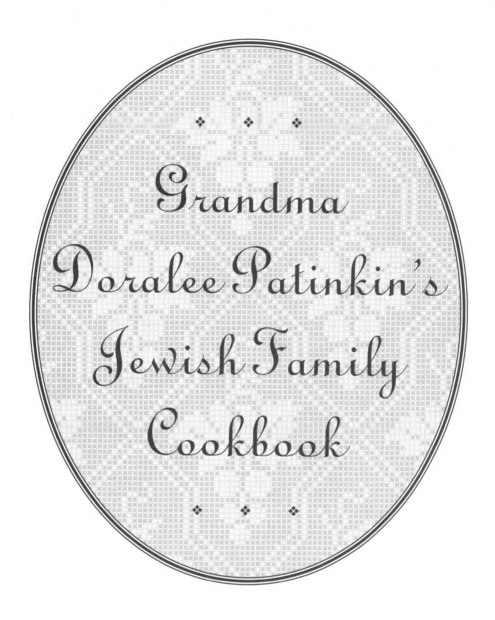

Grandma Doralee Patinkin's Jewish Family Cookbook

DORALEE PATINKIN RUBIN

INTRODUCTION BY MANDY PATINKIN

GRANDMA DORALEE PATINKIN'S JEWISH FAMILY COOKBOOK. Copyright ©
1997 by Doralee Patinkin Rubin. All rights reserved. Printed in the
United States of America. No part of this book may be used or repro-
duced in any manner whatsoever without written permission
except in the case of brief quotations embodied in critical articles or
reviews. For information, address St. Martin's Press, 175 Fifth
Avenue, New York, N.Y. 10010.

Library of Congress Cataloging-in-Publication Data

Rubin, Doralee Patinkin.
    Grandma Doralee Patinkin's Jewish family cookbook   :
more than 150 treasured recipes from my kitchen to yours   /
Doralee Patinkin Rubin.
        p.   cm.
    ISBN 0-312-16856-X (hc)
    ISBN 0-312-24445-2 (pbk)
    1. Cookery, Jewish.   I. Title.
TX724.R655   1997
641.5'676–dc21   97-20906
                                                                  CIP

First St. Martin's Griffin Edition: November 1999

THIS BOOK IS DEDICATED TO ISAAC AND GIDEON GRODY-PATINKIN;
LAINIE, AMANDA, AND LESLIE PATINKIN-RUBENSTEIN;
LAURIE, KARIE, AND DEBRA RUBIN; DAVID AND MATTHEW RUBIN;
BECKY AND JEREMY GIMBEL; AND DONNY AND
JONATHAN RUBIN—ALL MY GRANDCHILDREN.

IN MEMORY OF

Lester Don Patinkin,

1919–1972

Contents

Preface

My children, Marsha and Mandy, always thought I should record my recipes for posterity and for themselves. A holiday never passed that they didn't have me on the phone requesting advice on how to prepare a turkey or sweet potatoes or tzimmes or the potato latkes they loved so much as children. As their lives became more complicated and their interests diversified, these phone calls became more and more frequent, and so did their requests for me to write my recipes down.

One day, Mandy called and told me a computer and printer would be arriving soon, and that I had better get to work. When I finally began, I was amazed to find that after a full day of writing and testing recipes, I could still end up with nothing for dinner! It was then that I realized that cooking should always be as simple as possible. As a result, I've tried to present each recipe with the thought in mind that perhaps this is the cook's first experience and that success can be easily achieved.

While the recipes in this book are born of family, tradition, and a proud sense of heritage, this cookbook may not be appropriate for those who observe the laws of Kashrut, although most recipes could be easily adapted. However, those with a taste for old-fashioned, Jewish-style dishes like kugel, blintzes, latkes, chicken soup and knaidlach, plum kuchen, and more should not be disappointed with what follows. You will also find a touch of other ethnic cuisines such as Mexican, Italian, Greek, Oriental, and Mid-Eastern, which I delight in serving.

A word about kitchen equipment: I used to love to prowl the fancy housewares stores looking for the latest gadget on the market, the newest line of cookware, and the newest appliance. Today, I am shopped out, but I still believe you should have the best equipment available. Keep in mind that the best is not necessarily the most expensive. Modern kitchen equipment is available in many price ranges, so don't let price alone dictate your choices.

Because some of the recipes in this collection have been in use for decades, it was essential that I modify them to make them fit the health-conscious mood of our times. In most cases, I've given the recipe for the "real thing," including butter, salt, and sugar, among other ingredients, and I've also included ways to make them no-salt, low-fat, no-fat, and no-sugar. If you choose to cook without sugar, try substituting apple juice or orange juice concentrate and a small amount of artificial sweetener. To avoid using egg yolks, try egg substitutes plus some extra egg whites for most recipes. (See my "Helpful Hints" section for more details.)

Finally, I would like to emphasize that this is not a gourmet cookbook. I have always loved to cook and entertain, and this collection reflects a lifetime's worth, and in some cases, several generations' worth, of recipes. Many have become my signature dishes and are as old as the hills, family favorites that go back as many as fifty years. The memories of good times come back to me each time I prepare them.

I wrote this book so that my children and grandchildren would be able to say "Grandma always made this," and then know how to make it in their own kitchens for family dinners, dinner parties with friends, and special holiday celebrations.

In recent years, I have devoted most of my efforts to the dessert tables for my grand-children's Bar and Bat Mitzvah celebrations. My motto has become, "Have Cookies, Will Travel," and travel they do. From California to Nevada, to Chicago, and to New York. You will recognize, I am sure, many sweet favorites of your own. They are favorites because they have stood the test of time.

I hope you enjoy reading and using this collection as much as I have enjoyed preparing it.

—Doralee Patinkin Rubin

Special Thanks...

To my granddaughter, Becky Gimbel, for her help and patience in teaching me how to master the computer, and to my son-in-law Kenneth Gimbel, for his vigilance in computer troubleshooting;

To my daughters, Marsha Patinkin and Joanne Gimbel, without whose counsel and encouragement this book would not exist;

To my friends and relatives, who contributed recipes many years ago;

To my husband, Stan Rubin, for his infinite patience and understanding;

To Carla Glasser of the Betsy Nolan Literary Agency, who brought me to St. Martin's Press;

To my editor, Marian Lizzi of St. Martin's Press, who was most patient and cooperative with me;

To Steve Snider and the entire staff of St. Martin's Press, for being so thoughtful;

And last, but hardly least, to my son, Mandy, and my daughter-in-law, Kathryn Grody, who sent me the computer, told me to go to work, and wanted the world to buy their mother's cookbook. Without their help and guidance this book would never have come to fruition.

Plus a special thank-you to Todd Finnigan. How could I have managed without you!!

Introduction

BY MANDY PATINKIN

Reading my mom's cookbook makes me feel like I'm ten years old, sitting at the Passover table, just waiting for dessert. . . . Chocolate Sponge Cake–that was one of my favorites, and my mom would make this strawberry sauce, or a lemon sauce, that we loved to drench the cake in. . . .

This book is like taking a private tour through our family and friends, from the early fifties, and in some cases even before I was born, right up to the present. It's a trip to see the old favorites actually in print, like Hot Dogs and Baked Beans. I remember my mom always said, aside from adding the mustard and ketchup: Don't forget to put in a little brown sugar. I loved it then and I love it today. And then there's David Block's mother's recipe for tuna burgers that my mom changed a little. They are not only still one of my favorite things to eat, but they have also become a favorite of my kids.

Sure, my mom can make anything taste and look like it came out of a five-star restaurant, but frankly, I love just hunting through these pages looking for my childhood. That, for me, is one of the greatest things about this book: This part of my childhood isn't lost.

Let me tell you a bit about some of the characters you'll meet throughout my mom's book. There's Grandma Ida, who was my mom's mom, and Grandma Celia, who was my dad's mom. My Grandma Celia's gefilte fish is, as my sons would say, "awesome." You can try this brand or that from any store in the world, but you haven't lived until you've had Grandma Celia's gefilte fish. I had to have a piece of cooked carrot with every bite (I could take or leave the horseradish).

Aunt Ida and Aunt Lillian, my father's older sisters, were both great cooks. On occasion, I've given out recipes for Aunt Lillian's kichel at my concerts, and now my mom has given it to you. Then there was Aunt Lou, who was the frat mom to my dad's fraternity when he was at the University of Chicago. She was also my baby nurse when I was little.

Plus there was the inseparable foursome, made up of my mom and the wives of my dad's best buddies from the frat, Hy, Smitty, and Sid. Their wives, Shirley, Evy, and Bella, along with my mom, made up the group I think of as My Four Mothers. I was shocked to see that my mom included some of Bella's recipes, because when I was growing up I thought all she ate was a minimum of twelve ears of corn at any given sitting.

You'll hear about my cousin Barry, who is Aunt Lillian's youngest son. Barry will tell you that I was a pest growing up, and I will tell you that Barry beat me up at every family function. I'm now quite certain that, in one way or another, I begged for the beating. In fact, I think I loved provoking Barry and David (David is Aunt Ida's baby)– that is, I loved it until I got hurt, and I always got hurt.

Let me go back to Grandma Ida for a moment. What I remember most about her is *Rolly Polly, Rolly Polly, Rolly Polly.* Grandma Ida would take my wrist in her hands and roll it quickly back and forth between her palms, saying *Rolly Polly, Rolly Polly, Rolly Polly.* Well, the tradition has lived on, only now instead we say *Grandma Ida, Grandma Ida, Grandma Ida.*

There are many other characters you will meet in this book–my sister Marsha, my stepsister Joanne, my aunt June, my cousin Robin, to name a few.

As I flipped through the dessert section of this book, I thought, if you make these items and like them, you'll be dead before your time–but you'll have a great time getting there. And if you don't like them, send them to me and I'll eat them for you; I'll even give you my FedEx number.

My mother has always lived in the kitchen. It has been her kingdom, her palace, her meditation; but most of all it is her love and her passion. It's funny how as children we learn from our parents. I hope I swallowed the passion and love my mom displayed in her kitchen. And if I'm lucky enough to have any passion or love for what it is that I do in life, I'm certain a great deal of it was fed to me by my mother.

This is not just a cookbook; it is a true labor of love on many fronts. When I first sat down to read it, I was deeply moved. Who ever heard of anyone being moved by a cookbook? But I turned to my wife, Kathryn, and said, "This is my mom's life's work." I'm moved that it has been recorded, just like a play, a film, or a piece of music.

I like to flatter myself and think that my sister Marsha and I, and all my mom's grandchildren, are her true life's work, and indeed my mom will be the first to tell you we all are. But family aside, I've eaten in restaurants all over the world, and nobody's a better cook than my ma.

I want to thank Carla Glasser for selling this book to St. Martin's Press, Tom Poague for selling Carla Glasser to my mom and me, and Marian Lizzi and Steve Snider for their enthusiasm and gifts in making my dream for my mother a reality.

But most of all I want to thank my mom. You did all the work—not just for this book, but all through the years, and all your children and grandchildren will forever be grateful to you.

Love, Mandy

Helpful Hints

MEASUREMENTS

Today, we have the most modern equipment to help us operate efficiently in the kitchen, but how many of you remember when your grandmother never used standard measuring units? Instead of a tablespoon or two, it was an "eggshell full," and instead of a cup it was a "glass"–and we all know what kind of glass that was: a memorial or Yahrzeit glass that had burned out and been scoured, sterilized, and saved for just this new purpose in the kitchen.

It is most important to use the right measurements when cooking or baking.

Use glass measuring cups to measure any kind of liquid.

Use metal measuring cups to measure flour, sugar, shortening, and other solid ingredients.

Use measuring spoons to measure salt, spices, and other small-quantity ingredients.

LIQUID MEASUREMENTS
1 cup = 8 fluid ounces
2 cups = 16 fluid ounces
4 cups = 32 fluid ounces
2 cups = 1 pint
2 pints = 1 quart
1 quart = 4 cups
4 quarts = 1 gallon

ONE-POUND EQUIVALENTS
2 cups butter
4 cups flour
2 cups granulated sugar
3$\frac{1}{2}$ cups powdered sugar (packed)
2$\frac{1}{4}$ cups brown sugar (packed)

DRY MEASUREMENTS
3 teaspoons = 1 tablespoon
4 tablespoons = $\frac{1}{4}$ cup
16 tablespoons = 1 cup
2 tablespoons = 1 ounce
4 ounces = $\frac{1}{4}$ pound
16 ounces = 1 pound

TIPS FOR USING YOUR FOOD PROCESSOR

First of all, always refer to your manual. Most processors come with a shredding blade, a slicing blade, a steel blade, and a plastic blade.

Some of the blades are very sharp and one must be very careful when inserting or removing them.

A cardinal rule: Never try to remove the lid when the machine is running.

Additional blades with various functions are available from your processor dealer.

I, personally, still prefer using a good sharp knife for most of my slicing or chopping. However, there are maybe one or two recipes where I recommend double process-ing–that is using the shredding blade and then processing it again with the steel blade.

For almost all other functions, such as chopping or mixing, I use the steel blade. I rarely use the plastic blade, which is really best for sauces and very light batters.

Always use the on-off (pulse) motion. This motion allows you to watch the contents and helps you to obtain the right consistency. Rotate your bowl on and off if it does not have a switch.

In baking, when creaming butter, eggs, and sugar, start with a pulsing action until everything is incorporated, and then allow the machine to run for as long as neces-sary to obtain a light, thick, and creamy consistency.

Remember, the time necessary for a processor to achieve the proper result is consid-erably shorter than for an electric mixer.

When it is time to add the dry ingredients to a mixture in the processor, once again use the on-off pulse motion just long enough to incorporate the ingredients. At this point, do not overbeat, unless directions are otherwise, such as allowing the dough to form a ball. You then let the processor run until the mixture leaves the sides of the bowl and forms a ball.

Remember, there are no set speeds for your processor as there are for an electric mixer.

You will find many uses for your processor and will learn to be comfortable using it. Once you get the feel of this amazing machine, you'll wonder how you ever got by without one.

SUGAR SUBSTITUTES

When cooking with a sugar substitute, you should not use an aspartame product. The sugar substitute that contains saccharin is the preferred one for cooking, because it sustains the flavor better. Do not use liquid sugar substitutes in cooking or baking. The sweeteners can be purchased in bulk as well as in packets. Bulk packaging is more convenient if you use this item often.

Below are the suggested equivalents:

GRANULATED SUGAR	SUBSTITUTE
1/4 cup	1 teaspoon
1/3 cup	1 1/4 teaspoons
1/2 cup	2 teaspoons
1 cup	4 teaspoons

Please keep in mind that one of the best sugar substitutes is frozen apple juice—undiluted.

I always suggest using apple juice in cooking, with only a small amount of a substitute, as too much of a substitute can leave an aftertaste.

Delicious sugar-free dishes can be easily achieved if the above suggestions are followed.

BUTTER OR MARGARINE?

When a recipe calls for butter, this is always my first choice; however, you may always substitute margarine for butter, realizing that you are sacrificing some flavor.

Under no circumstances, however, should you substitute the "light" type of margarines or butter, whether in stick or tub form, for the real thing. The "light" types contain a great deal of water and will alter the consistency of your recipe considerably.

In certain recipes, you might consider using peanut or vegetable oil. Some recipes originally called for oil and worked out very nicely. For instance, in my mandelbrot, I always add a little oil. The end result is a little lighter and more crisp than most. It is all a matter of taste.

HERB BLENDS TO REPLACE SALT

I have found that by using certain combinations of herbs, I never miss the use of salt.

Sprinkle poultry or meat with garlic powder, curry powder, pepper, rosemary, paprika, and fresh lemon juice. Do not be afraid to use the curry powder. Blended with the other seasonings, it works miracles. Adjust the quantities according to taste. Salt can be kept to a minimum if you learn to use herbs and fresh lemon juice.

Here are a few basic combinations I've found are useful. After blending, keep in an airtight container and use as needed.

NO. 1

2 teaspoons garlic powder

1 teaspoon dried basil

1 teaspoon curry powder

1 teaspoon dried oregano

When using this combination, pour fresh lemon juice over meat or poultry.

NO. 2 PUNGENT

3 teaspoons dried basil

2 teaspoons savory

2 teaspoons celery seed

2 teaspoons ground cumin

2 teaspoons sage

2 teaspoons dried marjoram

1 teaspoon dried thyme

NO. 3 SPICY

1 teaspoon ground cloves

1 teaspoon pepper

1 teaspoon ground coriander

2 teaspoons paprika

1 teaspoon dried rosemary

VINEGAR SOURS MILK

For a taste much like sour cream or buttermilk, add 1 tablespoon white vinegar to 1 cup fresh milk. *Do not start with sour milk.*

Allow the mixture to sit at room temperature for at least 30 minutes.

EASY CLEANUP

To prevent foods from sticking to your outdoor grill, always spray the grill first with a vegetable cooking spray.

I also suggest doing this for all your cooking utensils, coated or plain, especially your stockpots when making soup. It makes cleanup much easier.

CENTERPIECES

I like to use ornamental kale, which is available in the produce section of your local supermarket and comes in pink, green, or white.

Anchor the bunch of kale in a florist's oasis, sitting in a shallow dish of water. Clip some leaves from the head of kale to fill in the gaps between the heads.

Candles may also be anchored in the oasis, depending upon the size of the centerpiece.

Take advantage of bunches of seasonal fresh vegetables, grouped together, to make very attractive centerpieces.

A FEW WORDS ABOUT THE HOLIDAYS

Holidays are a time for families and friends to gather and rejoice. What follows are some traditions our family has shared, and the important role that food plays in each one.

THE SHABBAT

The Shabbat (Sabbath) is our most important holiday, observed every Friday night and Saturday of the year, and has always been celebrated in our home. The table is beautifully set with lovely dishes and flowers. The Shabbat candles are waiting to be blessed. The kiddush cup (wine goblet) is ready for the prayer over the wine, and the challah (traditional egg bread) is draped with a beautiful cover, awaiting the blessing when we all break bread. A traditional Shabbat meal could consist of challah, gefilte fish, or chopped liver, soup and noodles, a potato kugel, a tzimmes, chicken or brisket, vegetables, and always dessert and tea.

THANKSGIVING

Thanksgiving dinners vary from family to family. I usually prepared the Thanksgiving dinner, and it was very traditional. Roast turkey, mashed potatoes, candied sweet potatoes, a vegetable casserole, two types of cranberry sauce, relishes, and old-fashioned pumpkin pie, among many other desserts. It's an occasion for great sharing and love.

HANUKKAH

Hanukkah is a holiday in which my children always delighted. The families were invited. The menorahs were lit. Presents were brought for all. We rigged up a tent over a table, with the gifts hidden behind. We used a fishing pole to "fish" for gifts. Imagine their delight when the children "fished" for just what they wanted. It became a tradition, after the opening of gifts, that the children moved all the furniture, and then put on a theatrical extravaganza for us. Certain things never seem to change. My grandchildren do the very same thing today. (It must be genetic!)

A Hanukkah meal would never be the same without potato latkes. So don't forget them!

PASSOVER

Passover immediately brings to mind all items necessary for the seder plate, such as charoses, horseradish, parsley, a roasted shankbone of lamb, and a roasted egg. These symbols are explained during the reading of the Haggadah. I always prepared large quantities of charoses, as it is to be eaten during the reading of the Haggadah, and any other time anyone wanted it during the week of Passover.

The main meal might consist of any of the traditional foods associated with a Shabbat (Sabbath) meal: gefilte fish, soup and knaidlach, chicken, brisket, potato kugel, and an assortment of Passover desserts.

ROSH HASHANAH

Rosh Hashanah, the beginning of a new year, may be celebrated with a big dinner the night before the first day; a dinner upon returning from temple after services; or a dinner at night. It varies from home to home. We greet the new year with sweet thoughts and hopes for a good and sweet year, and as guests enter, we usually serve sliced apples, the fruit of the earth, which we dip in honey.

The table or tables are set with beautiful dishes, lovely flowers, glowing candles, and, of course, a sumptuous meal is usually served. On Rosh Hashanah, it is customary to prepare some sweet dishes: carrot pudding, carrot or prune tzimmes, or a fruit compote. The rest of the menu is usually chosen from the traditional foods associated with the Shabbat (Sabbath).

YOM KIPPUR

Yom Kippur is a difficult time for some people because of the fasting, so we usually have a rather bland meal the night the holiday starts, fast all day on Yom Kippur, and upon returning from temple in the evening, gather with family and friends for a lavish dairy buffet: lox and bagels and cream cheese, sweet-and-sour fish, tuna salad, herring, noodle kugels, sliced cold vegetable platter, and always desserts.

All the recipes for foods served on these special days are listed in their proper section of this book. Your choices do not have to be my choices.

Happy holidays from our house to yours.

Appetizers

Egg Salad Party Mold

❖ ❖ ❖

IN THE DAYS OF BRIDAL LUNCHEONS, THIS WAS ALWAYS A
POPULAR PART OF THE BUFFET. EGG SALAD IS STILL ONE OF
MY ABSOLUTE FAVORITES, AS MY FAMILY WELL KNOWS.

Place the eggs in a food processor. Using the steel blade, process until finely chopped. Use on-off motion to avoid overprocessing. Transfer to a large bowl.

Combine eggs with the balance of ingredients, and pack firmly into a greased medium-size ring mold. Refrigerate for several hours.

Blend all the sauce ingredients and refrigerate until ready to use.

When ready to serve, unmold the egg salad on a serving platter and place the caviar sauce in a bowl in the center of the mold.

YIELD: 12 TO 18 SERVINGS

EGG SALAD:

18 *hard-boiled eggs*

1 *sweet onion, diced*

1/4 *cup chopped pimien-to*

1/3 *cup chili sauce*

1/4 *cup mayonnaise*

salt and pepper to taste

CAVIAR SAUCE:

2 *small jars red caviar*

2 *tablespoons mayonnaise*

2 *tablespoons chili sauce*

Sweet-and-Sour Meatballs

❖　❖　❖

IF YOUR FAMILY AND FRIENDS ARE LIKE MINE, THEY WILL
ALWAYS WANT MORE THAN ONE MEATBALL. SO I'VE INCLUDED
THREE VARIATIONS, WHICH DIFFER IN THE
SAUCE SEASONINGS.

MEATBALLS:

2　pounds ground meat

2　eggs

1　envelope onion soup
　mix

1/2　cup water

1/2　cup seasoned bread
　crumbs

1/2　cup ketchup or chili
　sauce

　salt and pepper to
　taste

Combine all the ingredients and roll into small balls. Set aside,
then choose one of the sauce recipes that follow.

SAUCE I:

1　bottle (Bennett's) chili
　sauce

1　chili sauce bottle
　filled with water

2/3　cup brown sugar

1　small bay leaf

3 to 4 black peppercorns

1　teaspoon salt

Place all the ingredients in a 6-quart Dutch oven and bring to a
boil. Reduce to a fast simmer and place the meatballs carefully
into the simmering liquid.

Cover and cook for about 2 hours. Uncover and continue cooking until sauce thickens.

YIELD: 12 SERVINGS

Place all the ingredients in a 6-quart Dutch oven and bring to a boil. Reduce to a fast simmer and place the meatballs carefully into the simmering liquid.

Cover and cook for about 2 hours. Uncover and continue cooking until sauce thickens.

YIELD: **12 SERVINGS**

SAUCE II:

1   bottle chili sauce

¹/₂ chili sauce bottle
     filled with water

1   10-ounce jar of grape
     jelly

Place all the ingredients in a 6-quart Dutch oven and bring to a boil. Reduce to a fast simmer and place the meatballs carefully into the simmering liquid.

Cover and cook for about 2 hours. Uncover and continue cooking until sauce thickens.

YIELD: **12 SERVINGS**

SAUCE III:

1   1-pound can whole
     cranberry sauce

1   cranberry sauce can
     filled with water

1   12-ounce bottle chili
     sauce

1   chili sauce bottle
     filled with water

1   tablespoon dried
     minced onion

6 to 8 black peppercorns

Chopped Herring

❖　❖　❖

THIS IS A TRADITIONAL APPETIZER, USUALLY SERVED AT
HOLIDAY TIME. IT'S WONDERFUL WITH RYE OR PUMPERNICKEL
ROUNDS, OR ASSORTED CRACKERS. THANK YOU,
MRS. TURNER.

1	32-ounce jar herring in wine sauce
1	large sweet onion, cut into chunks
2	semisweet apples, unpeeled, cut into chunks
4	large slices of rye bread, toasted and broken into pieces
1	tablespoon white wine vinegar
1	teaspoon sugar or 1 packet sugar substitute
6	hard-boiled eggs, whites only (optional)

Drain herring well, saving $1/4$ cup of the wine sauce.

Place herring and $1/4$ cup wine sauce in a food processor and process slightly.

Add balance of ingredients, except the hard-boiled egg whites, and process until finely chopped.

Add the hard-boiled egg whites (optional) and process lightly.

This should be made at least 2 days in advance so that flavors blend. Store in the refrigerator.

Note: Do not freeze. This will keep in the refrigerator for at least 2 weeks.

YIELD: 18 SERVINGS

Hot Cream Cheese Hors d'Oeuvres

❖   ❖   ❖

THIS WAS MANDY'S ABSOLUTE FAVORITE AS A YOUNG CHILD.
AT FAMILY DINNER PARTIES, WE HAD TO BE SURE HE LEFT
SOME FOR THE OTHERS. AS MY CHILDREN GREW OLDER,
I USED A FULL SLICE OF BREAD AND SERVED THIS FOR
LUNCH. MY GRANDCHILDREN NOW CLAMOR
FOR THIS APPETIZER.

Mix all the ingredients, except the paprika.

Cut rounds from fresh white bread and toast lightly on one side.

Spread cheese mixture on top, sprinkle with paprika, and just before serving, broil until puffed and brown.

YIELD: 12 ROUNDS OR 6 FULL SLICES

1	3-ounce package cream cheese
1/2	teaspoon baking powder
1	egg yolk
1 1/2	teaspoon grated onion (to taste)
	dash of salt
	paprika
12	rounds of white bread (use 6 slices)

Mushroom Squares

❖ ❖ ❖

THIS HAS RECEIVED RAVE REVIEWS. IT IS A NICE ADDITION TO
A BRUNCH. JUST CUT INTO LARGER PIECES.

12 ounces mushrooms,
sliced

1 medium onion

1 cup grated
Parmesan or
Cheddar cheese, or 8
ounces cream cheese

1/4 pound butter, melted

4 eggs

2 tablespoons chopped
fresh parsley

1/4 teaspoon garlic pow-
der, or 1 fresh garlic
clove, chopped

1/2 teaspoon curry pow-
der

2 1/2 cups seasoned stuffing mix, crushed

Preheat oven to 350°F.

Place all the ingredients in a food processor and pulse with on-
and-off movements carefully. It should be well blended.

Place in a greased 8- or 9-inch quiche dish or an 11 × 7-inch
Pyrex dish and bake for 20 minutes.

Cut into small wedges or squares and serve plain or with a
sweet-and-sour mustard sauce.

Note: Egg substitutes can be used.

YIELD: 8 TO 12 SERVINGS

GRANDMA DORALEE PATINKIN'S JEWISH FAMILY COOKBOOK

Mexicali Mold

❖ ❖ ❖

IF YOU LIKE GUACAMOLE, THIS IS A WINNER.

Place all the ingredients, with the exception of the gelatin, in a food processor and blend well.

Melt the gelatin over low heat or in the microwave for a few seconds. Add immediately to the above mixture.

Pour into a 9½-inch flan pan with a removable bottom and chill overnight, until very firm. Release from sides of pan, leaving the mold on the bottom. Place on platter and garnish with circles of diced black olives, diced green onions, and chopped zucchini or cucumber, starting with chopped tomatoes in the center.

A quiche dish can also be used and brought from the refrigerator to the table without unmolding.

This can be served with tortilla chips, crackers, or toasted pita triangles.

YIELD: **12 SERVINGS**

2 to 3 ripe avocados, peeled, pitted, and cut into pieces

1 tablespoon fresh lemon juice

1 small package Italian salad dressing mix

2 cups sour cream (regular, light, or fat-free)

3 tablespoons chopped fresh parsley

2 to 3 drops Tabasco sauce

1 4-ounce can chopped green chilies

1 envelope unflavored gelatin, dissolved in ¼ cup cold water

Miniature Cheese Popovers, or Gougères

❖ ❖ ❖

THIS IS AN ABSOLUTE DELIGHT WITH A GLASS OF WINE OR FAVORITE COCKTAIL BEFORE DINNER.

1   cup water

5   tablespoons butter

1   teaspoon salt

$^1/_4$ teaspoon ground pepper

$^1/_4$ teaspoon ground nutmeg

1   cup flour

1   cup grated Swiss or Gruyère cheese

5   extra-large eggs, at room temperature (very important)

In a medium-size saucepan, bring the water, butter, salt, pepper, and nutmeg to a boil. When butter has melted, add all the flour at once and beat with a wooden spoon for at least 1 minute, until mixture leaves sides of pan clean. Remove pan from heat.

Add cheese and beat until incorporated. Beat in 4 of the eggs, one by one, until thoroughly absorbed. Beat until mixture is smooth, shiny, and firm.

Drop by teaspoons onto a parchment-covered cookie sheet. Beat remaining egg with $^1/_2$ tablespoon water, then brush tops of unbaked puffs with egg wash.

Preheat oven to 425°F.

Bake in upper third of the oven for about 20 minutes, or until golden brown and doubled in size.

Remove from oven and serve.

These will keep in the refrigerator for days or can be frozen. Just warm in the toaster oven before serving.

YIELD: ABOUT 3 DOZEN

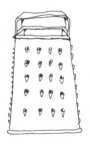

Artichoke Dip

❖ ❖ ❖

THIS IS TO DIE FOR! EVERYONE WILL GATHER AROUND
THIS IRRESISTIBLE DIP.

Preheat oven to 350°F.

In a food processor, blend the ingredients until slightly coarse.

Turn ingredients into a round baking dish and bake for 30 to 35 minutes.

Remove from oven and garnish with the marinated artichokes, cut into small pieces, placed around edge of baking dish. Sprinkle the chopped parsley inside the border of cut artichokes.

Serve while hot with tortilla chips, pita bread triangles, or crackers.

YIELD: 6 TO 8 SERVINGS

2   8-ounce jars marinated artichoke hearts, rinsed and drained

1   cup grated Parmesan cheese

$^{1}/_{2}$ cup mayonnaise

$^{1}/_{2}$ cup sour cream

1   8-ounce package cream cheese

$^{1}/_{2}$ teaspoon garlic powder

GARNISH:

1   8-ounce jar marinated artichokes, cut into small pieces

2   tablespoons chopped fresh parsley

Chopped Liver

❖ ❖ ❖

NO MORE CHICKEN FAT OR EGG YOLKS. THE SECRET IS IN
SIMMERING THE ONIONS. THE FLAVOR IS WONDERFUL!

1 very large sweet
   onion, cut into large
   pieces

3 tablespoons peanut
   oil

$^1/_2$ pound beef liver, cut
   into small chunks

2 hard-boiled eggs,
   whites only

$^1/_4$ teaspoon salt

$^1/_8$ teaspoon black
   pepper

1 small, very sweet
   onion, thinly sliced

   small crackers or
   cocktail rye

Heat the peanut oil in a large skillet. Add the large onion and
simmer on a low heat for an hour until slightly brown. Add the
chunks of liver and sauté just until the liver is done.

Transfer the liver and onions and oil remaining in the pan to a
food processor; add the salt and pepper and pulsate (on-off-on-
off) until smooth and thick. Do not overprocess. Add the egg
whites and process for just a few seconds.

Serve with the thinly sliced sweet onion and crackers or cocktail rye.

YIELD: 6 SERVINGS

Spinach Squares

❖　❖　❖

THIS IS A WINNER EVERY TIME! SERVE WITH MY SWEET-AND-SOUR MUSTARD SAUCE (SEE FOLLOWING RECIPE).

Preheat oven to 350°F.

In a food processor, blend all of the ingredients.

Pour into a greased 8½ × 11-inch oven-to-table baking dish, and bake for 25 minutes.

Allow to cool for 10 minutes and cut into squares.

YIELD: 25 TO 30 SQUARES

2　10-ounce packages frozen chopped spinach, drained

1½ cups herb-seasoned bread crumbs

1　cup grated Parmesan cheese

4　ounces cream cheese

5　eggs, well beaten

¼　pound melted butter or margarine

⅛　teaspoon nutmeg

Sweet-and-Sour Mustard Sauce

❖ ❖ ❖

THIS SAUCE IS WONDERFUL WITH A VARIETY OF APPETIZERS,
COLD MEATS, AND CHICKEN OR TURKEY SANDWICHES. I
USUALLY TRIPLE THE RECIPE AND KEEP IT IN THE
REFRIGERATOR FOR SEVERAL MONTHS.

¹/₃ cup dry mustard

¹/₂ cup white wine vinegar

¹/₂ cup sugar

1 egg yolk

Combine dry mustard and vinegar in a small bowl. Cover and let stand at room temperature overnight.

In a large saucepan, mix mustard and vinegar with the sugar and egg yolk. Blend very well. Over a medium-high heat, bring to a boil. Reduce to a low heat and stir until slightly thickened (5 to 10 minutes).

Pour into tightly covered jar and refrigerate.

Cocktail Dogs in Blankets

❖ ❖ ❖

THIS IS A WINNER EVERY TIME, BOTH WITH YOUNG AND OLD,
AND ALSO ALL THOSE WHO WILL THROW THEIR
DIETS TO THE WIND.

Preheat oven to 350°F.

Open the rolls and cut each crescent in half. Each roll will yield 16 pieces.

Place a hot dog or piece of one at the top of the crescent and roll toward the tip.

Place on a parchment-covered baking sheet and bake until lightly browned.

Serve with sauce of your choice—barbecue, salsa, mustard, or a sweet-and-sour mustard sauce.

These can be formed ahead and frozen. Bake as needed.

YIELD: 60 TO 64 PIECES

4   *packages crescent refrigerator rolls*

64   *cocktail hot dogs or 21 hot dogs cut into thirds*

Brunch

Apple Pancake

❖　❖　❖

THIS IS WONDERFUL AS A SUNDAY BREAKFAST, AS AN
ADDITION TO A BRUNCH MENU, OR JUST AS A VERY
SPECIAL DESSERT.

Preheat oven to 400°F. Spray a 12-inch quiche dish or a 13 × 9-inch pan. Melt butter in prepared dish or pan in oven. Mix apples, cinnamon, and sugars together. Add to hot butter and return to oven until butter sizzles. Toss once to make sure apples are well coated. Do not overcook.

Mix flour, baking powder, and salt together. Add milk or buttermilk, eggs, oil, and vanilla and stir just until dry ingredients are moistened. Do not overbeat.

Remove apples from oven and gently pour the batter over the apples. Sprinkle with the second 3 tablespoons of brown sugar. Return to oven and bake until puffed, edges golden, and apples tender, 25 to 35 minutes. Serve at once.

YIELD: 4 TO 6 SERVINGS

$1/4$	pound butter
3	Granny Smith apples, peeled and thinly sliced
$1/4$	teaspoon cinnamon
3	tablespoons white sugar
3	tablespoons brown sugar
1	cup flour
1	teaspoon baking powder
$1/2$	teaspoon salt
$1^1/2$	cups milk or buttermilk
6	eggs
2	tablespoons oil
1	teaspoon vanilla extract
3	tablespoons brown sugar

Blintzes

❖ ❖ ❖

WHEN MY CHILDREN WERE YOUNG, FROZEN BLINTZES WERE NOT AVAILABLE, SO WE MADE OUR OWN. INSTEAD OF FILLING THEM WITH CHEESE, I OFTEN USED SOLO APRICOT PASTRY FILLING (AVAILABLE IN THE KOSHER FOOD SECTION OF YOUR LOCAL SUPERMARKET). TRY IT.

BATTER:

4 eggs, well beaten

1 cup flour

1 teaspoon salt

2 cups milk

FILLING:

1 pound dry cottage or
   pot cheese

1 8-ounce package
   cream cheese

3 eggs

1 tablespoon butter,
   melted

1 teaspoon grated
   orange rind

3 tablespoons sugar

$1/2$ teaspoon cinnamon

$1/4$ teaspoon nutmeg

Combine all the filling ingredients and set aside.

For the batter, mix all the ingredients. Brush a 4- to 6-inch skillet lightly with butter and heat over medium to high heat. Do not allow butter to burn. Pour in just enough of the batter to coat the pan well, and cook until lightly brown on the bottom. Do not turn over. When done, flip onto a clean cloth or wax paper and continue with the rest of the batter. If it is possible to have two pans, it will proceed much faster.

Fill the brown side of the pancake with about 1 tablespoon of the filling and roll up, making sure you fold in the sides.

These can be prepared in advance of serving. May even be frozen. When ready to serve, melt some butter in a frying pan and brown slowly on all sides.

Serve with a fruit sauce or sour cream.

YIELD: 12 TO 18 BLINTZES

30   GRANDMA DORALEE PATINKIN'S JEWISH FAMILY COOKBOOK

Grandma's Blintz Pudding

❖ ❖ ❖

THIS HAS ALWAYS BEEN A SUCCESS. NO MORE STANDING AT
THE STOVE MAKING BLINTZES THE OLD-FASHIONED WAY. THIS
IS A SURE WINNER AND IS A FABULOUS ADDITION TO ANY
MEAL, ESPECIALLY A BRUNCH. I ASSEMBLE THIS IN ADVANCE,
FREEZE, AND BAKE WHEN READY TO SERVE.

Preheat oven to 350°F.

For the batter, cream butter and sugar well. Add the eggs, sour
cream, orange juice, and orange rind and blend well.
Incorporate the flour, to which you have added the baking powder and salt.

Combine the filling ingredients.

Grease an oven-to-table baking dish (approximately 13 × 9 inches) and pour in half the batter. Set balance aside.

Using a tablespoon, drop dollops of filling on top of batter, using
all of the mixture. Spread very lightly with a fork. Pour the balance of the batter over the top.

Bake for 50 to 60 minutes. When it is almost finished, remove
from oven, frost with the orange marmalade, and return to the
oven until it is bubbly. Allow to set for a few minutes.

YIELD: 12 SERVINGS

BATTER:

$^1/_3$	pound butter
$^1/_4$	cup sugar
6	eggs, or $1^1/_2$ cups egg substitute
$1^1/_2$	cups sour cream
$^1/_2$	cup orange juice
1	tablespoon fresh orange rind
1	cup flour
2	teaspoons baking powder
$^1/_2$	teaspoon salt

FILLING:

1	8-ounce package cream cheese (light, optional)
2	cups small-curd cottage cheese (low-fat, optional)
2	egg yolks, or $^1/_2$ cup egg substitute
3	tablespoons sugar
1	teaspoon vanilla extract
	orange marmalade

Easy Blintz Soufflé

❖ ❖ ❖

THIS WAS ALWAYS A BRUNCH FAVORITE AND SO EASY!

1   *package frozen blintzes (cheese or fruit)*

3   *eggs plus 2 egg whites, or ³/₄ cup egg substitute plus 2 egg whites*

¹/₂   *cup sour cream (light or fat-free can be substituted)*

¹/₄   *cup orange juice*

1   *teaspoon vanilla extract*

1¹/₂ *tablespoons sugar*

Preheat oven to 350°F.

Grease an 8¹/₂ × 11-inch ovenproof casserole. Place the frozen blintzes on the bottom.

Place the balance of the ingredients in a blender or food processor and blend until very creamy. Pour over the blintzes.

Bake for 35 to 45 minutes.

Serve with your favorite fruit topping.

YIELD: 4 TO 6 SERVINGS

Breakfast Soufflé

❖   ❖   ❖

I HAVE TAKEN THIS OLD RECIPE AND REDUCED THE FAT CONTENT AS MUCH AS POSSIBLE. IT WILL NOT BE AS RICH IN FLAVOR, BUT IS AN EXCELLENT SUBSTITUTE.

Combine all the ingredients except the margarine and the slices of bread. Blend well.

Melt the margarine in a 9 × 13-inch ovenproof casserole. Place half of the bread in the bottom of the casserole; pour half of the blended mixture over the bread. Layer the rest of the bread and finish with the balance of the mixture.

Refrigerate overnight.

Bake in a 325°F oven for 1 hour. Allow to set for at least 10 minutes before serving.

YIELD: 10 TO 12 SERVINGS

- ½ pound shredded Cheddar cheese (low fat)
- 4 egg whites
- 1 cup egg substitute (or 4 eggs)
- 2 cups low-fat or skim milk
- 2 teaspoons dry mustard
- 1 teaspoon Worcestershire sauce
- 6 ounces fresh mushrooms, sautéed in a little margarine
- 2 cups chopped marinated artichoke hearts

  chopped green chilies (optional, to taste)
- 4 tablespoons margarine
- 12 slices white bread, crusts removed

Frittata

❖ ❖ ❖

I FIRST BECAME ACQUAINTED WITH A FRITTATA MANY, MANY
YEARS AGO AT THE CORONA CAFE IN CHICAGO. I SERVE THIS
AT A BRUNCH, OR AS A MAIN COURSE FOR A LIGHT SUPPER,
WITH SOME SLICED TOMATOES AND CUCUMBERS, BAGELS, AND
BIALYS. ABSOLUTELY DELICIOUS!

12 ounces fresh mushrooms, sliced	Preheat oven to 400°F.
4 small zucchini, sliced	Grease a large ovenproof frying pan (one with a wooden handle) with some olive oil and heat on top of stove. Add the mushrooms, zucchini, red pepper, and onion and sauté for about 8 minutes.
1 large red bell pepper, diced	
1 large onion, sliced	
8 eggs, or 2 cups egg substitute	While the vegetables are cooking, beat the eggs or egg substitute with a whisk, and add all the seasonings.
1 teaspoon curry powder	
1 teaspoon dried basil or a mixed herb blend	Pour the eggs or egg substitute over the cooked vegetables and place over low heat for a few minutes until it starts to set.
1 teaspoon salt	
1/2 teaspoon white pepper	Remove from stove and place in oven for 15 to 20 minutes, or until the top starts to brown.
pineapple or raspberry salsa, heated	Serve with a warm pineapple or raspberry salsa.

YIELD: 6 SERVINGS

Eggs with Onions, Potatoes, and Salami

❖ ❖ ❖

WHEN I WAS YOUNG, AND WE HAD NOT YET HEARD OF
CHOLESTEROL, MY MOTHER, GRANDMA IDA, OFTEN MADE
THIS. SERVE THIS WITH SLICED TOMATOES, BAGELS OR
BIALYS, AND DREAM OF DAYS LONG GONE.

I have no exact amounts to give you, but this is what you do:

Boil some red potatoes. Cool and skin them. Cut them into chunks or slices. Slice a few onions and as much salami as you want.

Beat 6 to 8 eggs very well.

In a large skillet, heat some oil. Add the onions and fry until tender. Add the potatoes and allow them to get a little crisp. Add the sliced salami to the potatoes and onions and fry for a few seconds on both sides. Pour the beaten eggs over everything. Cook until the eggs are set.

YIELD: 4 SERVINGS

Grandma Doralee's French Toast

❖   ❖   ❖

THIS WAS ALWAYS A REQUEST OF MY GRANDCHILDREN WHEN
THEY CAME TO VISIT—BREAKFAST, LUNCH, OR DINNER.

6   eggs, or 1¹/₂ cups egg
    substitute

¹/₂   cup orange juice

1   teaspoon salt

¹/₈   teaspoon cloves

¹/₂   teaspoon cinnamon

1   1³/₄-pound challah
    (egg bread), cut into
    ³/₄-inch slices

    peanut oil for frying

Combine eggs, orange juice, salt, cloves, and cinnamon. Blend well. Soak each piece of bread in liquid. Place in a large Pyrex dish and pour remaining liquid over bread. Soak several hours or overnight.

Coat a large skillet with vegetable spray. This will prevent sticking. Add peanut oil and heat until hot. Fry each piece until golden brown and crispy on each side, adding additional oil as needed. Remove and place on paper toweling, which will absorb the oil. Transfer to an ovenproof serving platter. Place in a 275°F oven, adding slices as they are finished.

Serve with syrup, preserves, powdered sugar, or sliced fresh fruit, or any combination of the above.

Leftovers can be frozen and heated in the microwave or toaster oven.

Grandma Hatty's Noodle Pudding

❖ ❖ ❖

A TRADITIONAL GRODY FAMILY FAVORITE THAT HAS NOW
BECOME A GRODY-PATINKIN FAMILY FAVORITE! KATHRYN AND
MANDY'S CHILDREN LOVE THIS.

Preheat oven to 350°F.

Blend all the ingredients except the noodles in a processor or electric mixer until thick and creamy.

Place all of the cooked noodles in a well-greased 8½ × 11-inch baking dish. Pour the blended mixture over the noodles.

Bake for approximately 45 minutes, or until a golden brown.

YIELD: 8 SERVINGS

³/₄ pound unsalted butter

5 whole eggs

4 ounces cream cheese

1 cup sour cream

1 cup honey

12 to 16 ounces semi-broad noodles (cooked according to instructions on package, drained, and rinsed with cold water)

Velvet Noodle Pudding

❖ ❖ ❖

MELTS IN YOUR MOUTH! THIS WAS STANDARD FARE AT MY
AUNT ETHEL'S HOUSE WHEN WE WERE YOUNG.
SIMPLE AND YUMMY.

¹/₄ pound butter, melted

1 8-ounce package cream cheese

4 eggs

¹/₂ cup sugar

1 cup whole milk

1 teaspoon vanilla extract

8 ounces semi-broad noodles (cooked according to directions on package, drained, and rinsed with cold water)

TOPPING:

1 cup crushed corn flakes

¹/₂ teaspoon cinnamon

2 tablespoons sugar

2 tablespoons butter, melted

Preheat oven to 350°F.

In a food processor or electric mixer, blend butter, cream cheese, and eggs. Add sugar, milk, and vanilla. Blend well. Transfer to a large bowl and add the cooked noodles. Blend. Pour into a greased oven-to-table 8¹/₂ × 11-inch serving dish.

Combine topping ingredients and spread over noodles. Bake for 1 hour.

YIELD: 6 TO 8 SERVINGS

Orange Noodle Pudding

❖ ❖ ❖

THIS IS MY FAVORITE KUGEL.
WHEN I DO NOT HAVE TO WORRY ABOUT THE FAT-FREE AND
SUGAR-FREE GUESTS, THIS IS THE KUGEL I PREFER TO MAKE.
THANK YOU, EVIE LEEDS.

Preheat oven to 350°F.

Beat the 6 egg whites into peaks and set aside.

Place the orange in the food processor and process well. Add the balance of the ingredients, except the noodles and preserves, and process well.

Place the cooked noodles in a large bowl. Add the orange mixture and mix well. Fold in the beaten egg whites.

Pour into a large oven-to-table serving dish about 8½ × 11 inches and bake for 45 minutes. Spread with orange preserves and return to oven until bubbly, about 15 minutes.

YIELD: 8 TO 10 SERVINGS

6   eggs, separated (room temperature)

1   navel orange, rind and all

1   cup sugar

2   cups sour cream

1   cup orange juice

¼   pound butter, melted

2   teaspoons vanilla extract

2   teaspoons salt

1   pound semi-broad noodles (cooked according to instructions on package, drained, and rinsed with cold water)

    orange or apricot preserves

Dairy-Free Noodle Pudding

❖   ❖   ❖

THIS IS NOT ONLY DAIRY-FREE, BUT CAN BE MADE SUGAR-FREE. I HAVE GIVEN YOU THE OPTIONS. AS I HAVE SAID, NECESSITY IS THE MOTHER OF INVENTION. THUS, THIS LEGAL AND STILL DELICIOUS NOODLE PUDDING. HOPE YOU LIKE IT.

1/4 pound corn oil margarine, melted

1 1/4 cups sugar (or 2 tablespoons Sweet 'n Low)

4 eggs, separated (or 1 cup egg substitute plus 4 egg whites)

1 20-ounce can crushed pineapple, drained

2 cups apple-apricot sauce or cinnamon apple sauce

1 teaspoon cinnamon

1 teaspoon orange rind

1/4 teaspoon ground cloves

salt to taste

1 pound No-Yolk noodles (cooked according to directions on package, drained, and rinsed with cold water)

raisins (optional)

sugar-free apricot or orange preserves

Preheat oven to 350°F.

In a large bowl, combine all the ingredients except the egg whites and preserves.

Beat the 4 egg whites until they form peaks and fold into the noodle mixture.

Pour into a greased 9 × 13-inch Pyrex baking dish.

Bake for 35 minutes. Remove from oven and frost with sugar-free apricot or orange preserves and return to oven for 25 minutes.

YIELD: 10 TO 12 SERVINGS

GRANDMA DORALEE PATINKIN'S JEWISH FAMILY COOKBOOK

Pumpkin Bread

❖   ❖   ❖

THIS IS GREAT WITH CREAM CHEESE, AT THANKSGIVING
OR ANY TIME OF THE YEAR.

Combine margarine or butter and sugar and cream well. Add eggs and beat until light and fluffy. Add the vanilla and pumpkin and blend. Combine all dry ingredients and add to the eggs, butter, and sugar. Add the chopped nuts and raisins and mix well.

Pour into 5 well-greased small aluminum foil loaf pans. If you prefer a large loaf, this recipe will make 2 large loaves (9 × 5 × 3 inches).

Preheat oven to 350°F. Bake for 55 to 60 minutes for the small loaves. For the larger loaves, increase the baking time slightly. Test with a toothpick. When it comes out clean, cake is ready to remove from oven.

11	tablespoons margarine or butter
$2^2/_3$	cups sugar
4	eggs
2	teaspoons vanilla extract
1	1-pound can pumpkin plus $^2/_3$ cup water
$3^1/_3$	cups flour
2	teaspoons baking soda
$^1/_2$	teaspoon baking powder
$^1/_2$	teaspoon salt
2	teaspoons cinnamon
2	scant teaspoons ground cloves
1	cup chopped nuts
$^2/_3$	cup raisins

Lemon Bread

❖ ❖ ❖

THIS HAS A MARVELOUS, LEMONY FLAVOR.

1/4	pound margarine or butter
1	cup sugar
2	eggs
1/2	cup milk
1 1/4	cups flour
1	teaspoon baking powder
1/2	teaspoon salt
1/2	cup chopped nuts
2	heaping teaspoons fresh lemon rind

GLAZE:

1/4	cup sugar
	juice of 1 lemon

Using a food processor, combine butter, sugar, eggs, milk, and lemon rind. Combine the flour, baking powder, salt, and nuts. Add to the food processor, incorporating with short pulsing motions. Do not overprocess.

Pour into a large loaf pan (9 × 5 × 3 inches) and bake for 1 hour, or until done.

Melt sugar and lemon together over medium heat until a syrup forms. Remove bread from oven and, while still warm, pour the glaze over the loaf. Puncture the top of the cake so glaze will penetrate.

Bran Spice Muffins

❖ ❖ ❖

START YOUR DAY WITH TWO OF THESE AND A CUP OF COFFEE—YUMMY!

Preheat oven to 400°F.

Combine cereal, molasses, and milk. Allow to stand for 15 minutes. Add oil and egg and blend well. Add raisins and applesauce and mix thoroughly.

Combine all dry ingredients and add to mixture. Mix well.

Fill well-greased 2-inch miniature muffin tins almost to the top.

Bake for 15 minutes. Cool in tins.

These freeze beautifully. When ready to eat, pop into the microwave on high for a few seconds. Do not overheat, they will become tough. If you prefer, use your toaster oven.

YIELD: 36 MUFFINS

2	cups Kellogg's All Bran Cereal
¹/₂	cup molasses
1¹/₂	cups milk
2	tablespoons vegetable oil
1	egg, well beaten
1	cup raisins
1	cup applesauce
1¹/₄	cups sifted flour
¹/₂	teaspoon salt
1	teaspoon baking soda
1¹/₂	teaspoons cinnamon
³/₄	teaspoon ground ginger
¹/₂	teaspoon ground cloves

Soups

Grandma Doralee's Chicken Soup

❖ ❖ ❖

IT'S GOOD FOR WHATEVER AILS YOU! TRY THIS WITH MATZO BALLS, USING THE RECIPE THAT FOLLOWS. CHICKEN SOUP WITH MATZO BALLS WAS ALWAYS PART OF A HOLIDAY MEAL IN OUR HOME.

Place the chicken in a very large stockpot with enough water to cover. Bring to a hard boil and skim off the top. Add all the vegetables and seasonings. Bring to a boil once again and then reduce heat to low and cook for about 2½ hours.

Remove the chicken and serve as you wish. Remove the vegetables, separating the carrots from the rest, and strain the soup. In order to remove the fat, I suggest using a gravy separator or placing the soup in the freezer for a short while, allowing the fat to rise.

As you know, clear chicken soup can be served many ways: with noodles, matzo balls, kreplach, etc. However, you may purée the vegetables you have removed and return them to the broth. This will only enhance the flavor. Some prefer only the carrots.

For chicken in the pot: Remove chicken meat from the bones and serve in large bowls of soup with matzo balls or noodles, or both, etc.

YIELD: 16 SERVINGS

1   large stewing chicken

1   large onion, peeled and halved

1   large rutabaga, peeled and halved

1   large turnip, peeled and halved

3   medium parsnips, peeled and halved

12 large carrots, peeled and cut into chunks

6   stalks of celery, cut into large pieces

1   bunch of parsley

3   garlic cloves

1   teaspoon curry powder

1   teaspoon mild Hungarian paprika

1   teaspoon kosher salt

dash of white pepper

Old-Fashioned Vegetable Soup

❖ ❖ ❖

WHEN MANDY WAS YOUNG, HE PREFERRED CAMPBELL'S VEGETARIAN SOUP TO MINE. HERE'S WHAT HE WAS MISSING! I ALWAYS KEEP A SUPPLY IN THE FREEZER.

In a large stockpot, combine all ingredients. Bring to a hard boil. Reduce heat to low, and allow to cook for about 1 hour. Test to see if beans are tender. Do not hesitate to add more liquid, if needed. Adjust seasonings.

YIELD: 3 TO 4 QUARTS

4 quarts chicken or beef stock, or the equivalent of a vegetarian stock (for a vegetarian stock, I prefer the kosher instant soup powders)

6 celery stalks, cut up

1 large onion, cut into small chunks

1 bunch of carrots, cut into small chunks

1/2 pound fresh string beans, cut into thirds

1 turnip, cut into small chunks

1 rutabaga, cut into small chunks

1 large sweet potato, cut into small chunks

1 cup chopped fresh parsley

1 parsnip, cut into small pieces

1 cup baby lima beans (which have been soaked overnight)

1/2 cup red kidney beans (which have been soaked overnight)

1/2 cup farfel type of pasta

4 medium zucchini, sliced

3 fresh tomatoes, cut into small chunks

8 halves of sun-dried tomatoes, cut into small pieces

1 teaspoon sweet paprika

1 teaspoon salt

1/2 teaspoon white pepper

1 teaspoon garlic powder

1/2 teaspoon turmeric

Matzo Balls (Knaidlach)

❖   ❖   ❖

As light as a feather! Perfect in my chicken soup.

Blend the eggs and oil together, but do not beat.

Add the balance of the ingredients except the chicken soup mix; blend well with a fork.

Place in the refrigerator for at least 15 minutes.

In a large pot, bring 3 quarts of water to a boil and add the instant chicken soup mix. Simmer slowly.

Using a teaspoonful at a time, form into small balls about the size of a walnut and drop into the boiling water. Cover and boil on low heat for at least 30 minutes. Allow to cool in the liquid, then gently remove to a flat container.

These can be frozen. Freeze on a flat sheet and then place in a heavy freezer bag. To reheat, drop in chicken soup and heat until ready to serve.

YIELD: 18 SMALL MATZO BALLS

Cholesterol Note: I do not recommend using egg substitute in this recipe. However, instead of 2 whole eggs, use 1 whole egg and 1 egg white only. Handle gently.

2	whole eggs
$^1/_4$	cup oil (I prefer olive oil)
1	teaspoon salt
$^1/_4$	teaspoon nutmeg
$^1/_4$	teaspoon garlic powder
$^1/_4$	teaspoon onion powder
$^1/_2$	cup matzo meal
2	tablespoons water
2	tablespoons instant chicken soup mix

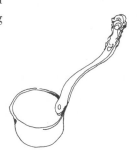

Gazpacho

❖ ❖ ❖

2 garlic cloves

1 large English cucumber, peeled and cut into chunks

2 very ripe large tomatoes, cut up

¹/₂ green bell pepper, cut into large pieces

3 celery stalks, cut into large pieces

1 lemon, juice and grated rind

4 tablespoons fresh parsley

³/₄ cup spicy V-8 vegetable juice

³/₄ cup regular V-8 vegetable juice

¹/₂ teaspoon dried basil leaves

¹/₄ teaspoon dried oregano

¹/₄ teaspoon dried cilantro

¹/₂ teaspoon curry powder

1 teaspoon Worcestershire sauce

1 small sweet onion

few drops of Tabasco sauce (optional)

THIS IS A WONDERFUL WARM WEATHER SOUP. ONE OF MY FAVORITES. A BOWL OF THIS AND SOME TORTILLA CHIPS—"¡MUY BIEN!"

Place all the vegetables in a food processor; using your steel blade, process with a slow pulsating motion until very thick but not watery. Add the balance of the ingredients, except Tabasco, and blend for just a few seconds.

Taste to adjust flavor, adding Tabasco to taste.

Refrigerate for at least 8 hours before serving. This will allow flavors to blend.

YIELD: 10 SERVINGS

Carrot-Zucchini Soup

❖ ❖ ❖

I CONSIDER THIS A REAL WINNER. DURING THE SUMMER,
I SERVE IT COLD. IN THE WINTER, I SERVE IT HOT.

Using the food processor, shred all the vegetables.

Grease a 4- to 6-quart pot. Melt butter or margarine and transfer vegetable mixture to pot. Sauté until soft. Should you prefer to sauté in a little chicken broth, you may do so. Add all the seasonings and parsley and return to the food processor. Process to a coarse consistency.

Return mixture to pot and add the chicken stock. Bring to a soft boil for about 5 minutes. Remove from stove. If you prefer a thinner consistency, adjust with additional chicken stock.

This may be served hot or cold.

This also freezes well.

Note: You may use all carrots (8) plus the potato or all zucchini (8) plus the potato.

YIELD: 18 TO 20 SERVINGS

4   large carrots, peeled

4   medium zucchini

1   medium onion

1   large garlic clove

1   large white potato

4   tablespoons butter or margarine

¹/₄   teaspoon salt

¹/₈   teaspoon ground cardamom

¹/₂   teaspoon curry powder

¹/₄   teaspoon nutmeg

  dash of white pepper

¹/₈   teaspoon turmeric

¹/₂   teaspoon parsley

  dash of paprika

6 to 8 cups defatted chicken stock

Beet Borscht

❖   ❖   ❖

WONDERFUL ON A WARM SUMMER DAY.

2	16-ounce cans sliced beets and juice
1	cup cold water
1/2	cup fresh lemon juice
4	teaspoons sugar (or 2 packets sugar substitute)
1	teaspoon salt
	sour cream or yogurt
	diced cucumber

Place all ingredients, except sour cream and cucumber, in a blender and process until all beet slices are pulverized. Borscht will be rather thick.

Chill.

Serve with sour cream or yogurt and diced cucumber.

YIELD: 10 SERVINGS

Spinach Borscht

❖   ❖   ❖

THIS IS AN OLD FAMILY FAVORITE, ESPECIALLY OF MINE.

Place frozen spinach, lemon juice, salt, and water into a 4-quart pot. Bring to a boil and allow it to simmer for about 5 minutes.

Remove from stove and add either chives (frozen or fresh) or chopped green onions.

Serve cold. Mix with yogurt or sour cream and a chopped hard-boiled egg.

YIELD: 8 TO 10 SERVINGS

1	10-ounce package *frozen chopped spinach*
	juice of 2 lemons
1½	*teaspoons salt*
8	*cups water*
	chives or green onions
	sour cream or yogurt
	hard-boiled eggs (optional)

Cold Cucumber Soup

❖   ❖   ❖

A SUMMER TREAT!

2   cups peeled and seed-
    ed cucumber chunks
    (I prefer European
    cucumbers)

1   garlic clove

1   tablespoon chives

3   sprigs fresh dill

2   tablespoons olive oil

    salt and pepper to
    taste

1   cup defatted chicken
    broth

1/2 cup mocha mix

1/4 cup fresh lemon juice

1   teaspoon prepared
    horseradish
    (optional)

    finely chopped
    cucumbers

    grated lemon rind

Blend the cucumber, garlic, chives, dill, oil, and salt and pepper in a food processor until coarse. Add the chicken broth, mocha mix, lemon juice, and horseradish. Blend well and serve cold. Garnish with finely chopped cucumbers and grated lemon rind.

YIELD: 6 SERVINGS

Salads

Grandma Doralee's Chicken Salad

❖ ❖ ❖

THE NUTS MAKE THE DIFFERENCE! MANDY LOVES THE CURRY.

Combine the chicken, celery, nuts, salt, and pepper. Dissolve the curry powder in the mayonnaise and add to the chicken mixture.

Blend all of the ingredients and chill. Adjust seasonings, and if you like a very moist salad, add more dressing.

YIELD: 4 TO 6 SERVINGS

2 to 3 cups cubed cooked breast of chicken

1 cup diced celery

1/2 cup walnuts or toasted pine nuts, very finely chopped

1 teaspoon salt

1/8 teaspoon white pepper

2 teaspoons curry powder

1/2 cup low- or no-fat mayonnaise

Oriental Chicken Salad

❖　❖　❖

THIS IS MY VERSION OF A VERY POPULAR SALAD. TRY
THIS WITH THE ORIENTAL DRESSING RECIPE ON
THE OPPOSITE PAGE.

*3 to 4 cups cubed cooked
chicken, skinned and
boned*

*2　red bell peppers, seed-
ed and cut into strips*

*1 to 2 heads Chinese cab-
bage, shredded*

*¹/₂　pound fresh snow
peas, strings removed,
cut diagonally*

*¹/₂　cup chopped cilantro
(optional)*

*6　ounces cellophane
noodles (see page 138
for instructions)*

*¹/₂　cup (or more) toasted
slivered or sliced
almonds*

Toss all the ingredients together and, just before serving, toss
with your favorite oriental salad dressing, or use the dressing
recipe that follows.

I have included a few dressings in this book, but there are some
excellent dressings available at your supermarket or your
favorite gourmet food shop.

Hint: To save time, cube the chicken ahead and store in a zippered plastic bag. Also, cut the vegetables and store in another
bag. Always be careful to remove all the air when sealing the
bag.

YIELD: **6 SERVINGS**

Oriental Dressing

❖　❖　❖

PERFECT FOR A CHICKEN SALAD OR CABBAGE SLAW. IF MAKING SLAW, I SUGGEST YOU USE SAVOY OR NAPA CABBAGE.

In a food processor or blender, combine all the ingredients and blend well. Adjust flavor according to your taste.

YIELD: ABOUT 1 CUP

1　6- or 7-ounce jar of plum sauce

2　teaspoons dry mustard

4　tablespoons seasoned rice vinegar

4　tablespoons sesame oil

4　tablespoons sugar, or $^3/_4$ teaspoon Sweet 'n Low

2　large garlic cloves

2 to 3 teaspoons light soy sauce

Antipasto Salad

❖　❖　❖

I BELIEVE THIS ORIGINALLY CAME FROM AUNT JUNE.

Combine all the ingredients. Pour the following marinade over
the salad and allow to marinate for a day or two.

1　pound green beans, cut and blanched	1　jar stuffed green olives, sliced	1　red bell pepper, chopped
1　large head cauliflower, separated	1　6-ounce can pitted black olives	1　yellow bell pepper, chopped
1　large bunch of broccoli, separated	3　cups artichoke hearts (canned)	1　pound raw mushrooms, sliced
1　bunch of green onions, minced	1　4-ounce jar sliced pimiento	
1　bunch of celery, chopped	1　green bell pepper, chopped	

MARINADE FOR RAW
VEGETABLES:

1　cup salad oil (I prefer
half olive oil, half
salad oil)

1/3　cup red wine vinegar

1　tablespoon honey

1　tablespoon sweet rel-
ish

　salt and pepper, to
taste

Combine all the ingredients and mix well.

YIELD: **12 TO 16 SERVINGS**

Mediterranean Salad

❖ ❖ ❖

I LOVE FETA CHEESE!

Place mashed garlic in a bowl and add the salt, lemon juice, olive oil, and pepper. Blend well. Add the remaining ingredients, except the tomatoes, and blend once again. Add the tomatoes just before serving and toss gently.

Adjust seasonings

Serve with toasted pita triangles.

YIELD: **4 SERVINGS**

1   garlic clove, peeled and mashed into a paste

½   teaspoon salt, preferably kosher, to taste

2   tablespoons fresh lemon juice

1 to 2 tablespoons extra-virgin olive oil

   ground pepper, to taste

½   English cucumber, peeled and diced (about 1½ cups)

2   ounces coarsely crumbled feta cheese

8   green onions, trimmed and chopped

¼   cup chopped fresh mint (optional)

¼   cup chopped fresh parsley

2   very large tomatoes, seeded and diced (about 2 cups)

Broccoli Salad

❖　❖　❖

THIS SALAD LOOKS AS GOOD AS IT TASTES! FROM THE
KITCHEN OF LESLIE WASSERMAN JACOBS.

*1 to 2 large hearts of
broccoli, separated
into florets*

*2   10-ounce packages
frozen petite peas*

*4 to 5 Roma tomatoes,
sliced or quartered
(or enough tomato
pieces to circle the
edge of the bowl)*

Marinate the broccoli florets and petite peas separately for at
least one day in a good red wine vinaigrette dressing. Do not
marinate the tomatoes.

Just before serving, combine the peas and the broccoli in a wide
bowl. Place the cut tomatoes around the sides of the bowl.

YIELD: 12 SERVINGS

Carrot Salad

❖   ❖   ❖

CARROTS ARE A VERY IMPORTANT SOURCE OF VITAMINS. HEALTHY AND DELICIOUS.

Using the shredding blade in your processor, process the carrots and transfer to a large bowl.

Toast the nuts in your toaster oven at 250°F. Watch very carefully, stirring them occasionally. When cool add with raisins to shredded carrots.

Add all the remaining ingredients and mix well. Adjust seasonings, if necessary, and refrigerate for a few hours.

YIELD: 6 TO 8 SERVINGS

1   *pound fresh carrots, shredded*

1   *cup golden or dark raisins*

1   *cup toasted pine nuts or toasted slivered almonds*

$^1/_2$ *cup fresh lemon juice*

1 to 2 *tablespoons mayonnaise*

$^1/_4$ *teaspoon salt*

$^1/_4$ *teaspoon ground cloves*

$^1/_8$ *teaspoon ground nutmeg*

$^1/_8$ *teaspoon ground ginger*

Three-Bean Salad

❖ ❖ ❖

THIS WAS ALWAYS A FAVORITE IN THE PATINKIN FAMILY. I
BELIEVE THIS WAS ORIGINALLY AUNT LILLIAN'S RECIPE.

1   27-ounce can kidney
    beans

1   16-ounce can cut
    green beans

1   16-ounce can garban-
    zo beans or wax
    beans (or both)

1   very large sweet
    onion, chopped

6   stalks of celery,
    chopped

$^1/_2$ cup sugar

1   teaspoon salt

$^1/_2$ cup white vinegar

Drain the beans, reserving $^1/_2$ cup of the liquid. Combine the
beans, onion, and celery and place in a deep refrigerator container.

Combine the bean liquid, sugar, salt, and vinegar in a saucepan.
Bring to a boil and pour over vegetables. Allow this to stand in
refrigerator for several days before serving.

YIELD: 12 SERVINGS

Marinated Cucumber Salad

❖　❖　❖

MY HUSBAND STAN'S FAVORITE SALAD.

Scrub (do not peel) and thinly slice the cucumbers. Place them in a bowl with just enough cold water to cover. Add enough seasoned rice vinegar to make the water sour, and then add sugar or sugar substitute to achieve the sweet-and-sour flavor. Salt to taste. Sprinkle with dill and toss.

A good rule of thumb is, for every 2 cups of water, add 4 tablespoons of seasoned rice vinegar, 2 teaspoons of sugar or the equivalent of a sugar substitute, always salting to taste.

At times, I will slice sweet onions very thin, as well as tomatoes, and add to the above.

The cucumbers and onions can be stored in the refrigerator for 2 days, but the tomatoes should be added a few hours before serving.

English or European cucumbers, if possible (they are not as watery and some say they are "burpless")

seasoned rice vinegar

sugar and salt

dried or fresh dill

Cucumber Cream Salad Mold

❖ ❖ ❖

ANOTHER ONE OF MY HUSBAND'S FAVORITES.

1   small package lime
    Jell-O

1   cup boiling water

2   tablespoons vinegar

1   teaspoon salt

1   teaspoon grated fresh
    onion, or 2 teaspoons
    dried onion

1   cup mayonnaise

    juice of ¹/₂ lemon

1   tablespoon dried dill

1   teaspoon dried
    cilantro

3   tablespoons cream-
    style white horse-
    radish

3   large cucumbers
    (English or European
    preferred) peeled,
    seeds removed,
    chopped in a food
    processor

1   envelope unflavored
    gelatin, dissolved in a
    little water

Dissolve lime Jell-O in the boiling water. Allow to cool slightly. Add all of the ingredients except the plain gelatin. Blend very well. Melt down the plain gelatin and add to the entire mixture. Blend once again.

Pour into a greased ring mold.

(I usually double this recipe.)

YIELD: 6 TO 8 SERVINGS

Pasta Salad

❖   ❖   ❖

A GREAT ADDITION TO A CASUAL MEAL.

Add all the vegetables and seasonings to the cooked and drained pasta. Toss very gently. Adjust seasonings carefully. Pasta absorbs the vinegar so a little more may be needed.

Refrigerate for several hours before serving.

YIELD: 6 SERVINGS

8   ounces small pasta (any type to make an attractive salad), cooked and drained

1   red bell pepper, cut into small pieces

1   green bell pepper, cut into small pieces

1   cup fresh snow peas, cut on the diagonal

1   small jicama, peeled and cut into small pieces

2   large fresh Roma tomatoes, sliced

1   cup broccoli florets

1   cup cauliflower florets

1   small can sliced black or green olives (or both)

1   small jar marinated artichoke hearts (drained)

^{1}/$_2$ teaspoon celery seed

1   teaspoon pepper

^{1}/$_2$ cup seasoned rice (or my Marinade for Raw Vegetables on page 79) vinegar

Gazpacho Mold

❖ ❖ ❖

THIS HAS BECOME A FAVORITE OF MINE AS WELL AS
MY GRANDSON, JEREMY GIMBEL.

1/2 cup chili sauce
   (chunky style)

1 cup ketchup

2 garlic cloves

1 green pepper

1 sweet onion

2 English cucumbers

2 large tomatoes

2 tablespoons white
   wine vinegar

3 to 4 drops of Tabasco
   sauce

1 tablespoon olive oil

2 teaspoons
   Worcestershire sauce

2 envelopes unflavored
   gelatin (dissolved in
   1/4 cup water)

Place all ingredients, except gelatin, in a processor. Process with a pulsing motion until coarsely chopped. Be careful not to allow mixture to become too loose.

Melt the gelatin over hot water or in the microwave for a few seconds and add to the vegetable mixture.

Pour into a greased medium-size mold and chill until firm. When ready to serve, unmold and garnish.

This is a marvelous appetizer, as well as a super addition to any meal. It can also be served in an attractive bowl.

If serving as an appetizer, bring out the tortilla chips.

Thousand-Island Potato Salad

❖ ❖ ❖

GREAT WITH HOT DOGS, HAMBURGERS, OR BARBECUED CHICKEN.

Combine the mayonnaise and chili sauce.

Combine the remaining ingredients and add the mayo-chili sauce mixture. Adjust seasonings.

Chill well, tossing a few times, allowing flavors to blend.

This can be made a day or two in advance of serving.

YIELD: 10 SERVINGS

1   cup mayonnaise (regular or fat-free)

1/2   cup chili sauce (chunky)

8   medium red potatoes or golden yukons (cooked and cooled, peeled, and cut into small chunks)

1   small red or white sweet onion, finely diced

1   red pepper, diced

1   cup diced celery

1   teaspoon salt

1/2   teaspoon curry powder

1/4   teaspoon pepper

Taco Salad

❖   ❖   ❖

FROM THE KITCHEN OF JOANNE GIMBEL.

1   *pound ground beef or turkey*

1   *package taco season- ing plus 1 cup water*

1   *27-ounce can kidney beans (washed and drained)*

1   *16-ounce can 3-bean salad (drained)*

1   *bunch green onions, chopped*

2   *large tomatoes, chopped*

¹/₄   *pound shredded sharp cheddar cheese*

1   *cup crushed nacho- flavor tortilla chips*

1   *large head of iceberg or romaine lettuce, shredded*

1   *bottle Kraft's Sweet and Spicy French Dressing*

Brown the beef or turkey and add taco seasoning and water. Simmer. Skim off fat. Cool.

Add the vegetables, cheese, chips, and the shredded lettuce. Add the dressing and toss well. Serve at once.

Great salad—a touch of Mexico!

YIELD: 6 TO 8 SERVINGS

Old-Fashioned Coleslaw

❖　❖　❖

A RECIPE THAT HAS STOOD THE TEST OF TIME!

Combine everything but cabbage. Pour dressing over the shredded cabbage and allow to marinate for several hours. Serve chilled.

YIELD: 6 SERVINGS

½ cup sour cream

1　teaspoon salt

　　dash of pepper

1　teaspoon celery seed

¼　teaspoon mustard seed

2　tablespoons champagne vinegar

1　teaspoon sugar

1　teaspoon Dijon mustard

1　teaspoon minced onion

1　large head white cabbage, finely shredded

Slim Slaw

❖ ❖ ❖

DELICIOUS, AND NOT A DIET-BUSTER.

1 head white cabbage

1 red bell pepper, chopped

6 ounces frozen apple juice, undiluted

²/₃ cup water

¹/₂ cup seasoned rice vinegar

¹/₃ cup white wine vinegar

¹/₂ teaspoon celery seed

salt and pepper, to taste

Shred the cabbage by hand or in the food processor. Add the red pepper. Combine all of the ingredients and toss well.

This should be made several hours in advance and chilled.

YIELD: 6 SERVINGS

Ambrosia

❖ ❖ ❖

THIS IS AN OLD FAMILY FAVORITE.

Combine all the ingredients and mix well.

Refrigerate overnight. The marshmallows should be dissolved into the mixture.

YIELD: **12 TO 16 SERVINGS**

1   cup sour cream

1   15-ounce can pineap-
    ple tidbits, drained

1   small bottle marachi-
    no cherries, drained

2   10½-ounce cans man-
    darin oranges,
    drained

1   10- to 12-ounce pack-
    age shredded coconut

½   pound chopped
    pecans or walnuts

2   cups miniature
    marshmallows

Pineapple Sour Cream Mold

❖   ❖   ❖

**THIS WAS ALWAYS A SUCCESS WHENEVER SERVED.
ESPECIALLY NICE FOR A BRIDAL LUNCHEON BUFFET.**

1 *large package lime Jell-O*	Dissolve Jell-O in boiling water and allow to cool.
1¾ *cups boiling water*	
2 *cups sour cream*	Add sour cream, pineapple, nuts, and cherries. Mix well. Pour into a greased mold and chill until firm.
1 *large can crushed pineapple (well drained)*	
¾ *cup chopped nuts (pecans or walnuts)*	Unmold, garnish, and serve.
1 *small bottle maraschino cherries*	YIELD: **12 SERVINGS**

Mandarin Orange Mold

❖ ❖ ❖

LOVED BY ONE AND ALL!

Dissolve the Jell-O in the boiling water. Add the cold liquid. Mix well. Add the orange sherbet and blend well with a whisk. Add the mandarin oranges.

Turn into a lightly greased mold or pretty bowl and chill until very firm.

YIELD: 8 TO 10 SERVINGS

1   large package orange or lemon Jell-O

1   cup boiling water

1   cup cold water, 7-Up, or ginger ale

1   pint orange sherbet

2   cans mandarin oranges (well drained)

Becky's Salad Dressing à la Romaine

❖ ❖ ❖

THIS HAS BECOME MY GRANDDAUGHTER BECKY'S FAVORITE DRESSING. HENCE THE NAME.

½	cup mayonnaise
½	cup sour cream
2	tablespoons grated Parmesan cheese
1	tablespoon fresh lemon juice
2	garlic cloves, crushed
½	teaspoon salt
⅛	teaspoon white pepper

Combine all the ingredients and refrigerate for several hours. Will keep in refrigerator for several days.

Serve over romaine, cut into bite-size pieces. Toss well.

Remember: Greens that are absolutely dry will hold the dressing better.

YIELD: 1 CUP DRESSING, ENOUGH FOR 12 SERVINGS

Caesar Salad Dressing

❖   ❖   ❖

THIS IS WONDERFUL AS A CHICKEN OR SHRIMP CAESAR,
ALSO. TO YOUR REGULAR CAESAR SALAD, JUST ADD HOT OR
COLD GRILLED CHICKEN OR HOT OR COLD GRILLED SHRIMP.

Mix all the ingredients together. When ready to serve, toss with
romaine lettuce and add grated Parmesan cheese and croutons.

YIELD: ABOUT 6 SERVINGS

$^1/_4$ cup olive oil

2   garlic cloves, crushed

4   teaspoons fresh lemon
    juice

$^1/_2$ teaspoon
    Worcestershire sauce

$^1/_4$ teaspoon fresh
    ground pepper

1   tablespoon chopped
    anchovies (you may
    use anchovy paste)

1   large head fresh
    romaine lettuce,
    washed and cut into
    pieces

$^1/_2$ cup grated Parmesan
    cheese

    seasoned croutons

Creamy Tofu Dressing

❖ ❖ ❖

**THIS IS A WONDERFUL CREAMY GARLIC DRESSING
AND SO LEGAL.**

¹/₄ pound firm tofu

1¹/₂ tablespoons balsamic
vinegar

2 garlic cloves, crushed

¹/₂ teaspoon Dijon mus-
tard

¹/₄ cup defatted chicken
stock or water

2 tablespoons olive oil

¹/₂ teaspoon salt

¹/₄ teaspoon freshly
ground black pepper

1¹/₂ tablespoons minced
fresh dill, basil, or
tarragon

In a food processor, combine tofu with vinegar, garlic, and mustard and process until smooth. Combine chicken stock with the oil and add to the purée, slowly. Add salt and pepper and blend.

Add the herbs just before serving.

YIELD: **1 CUP**

Marinade for Raw Vegetables

❖   ❖   ❖

THIS CAN BE USED FOR VEGETABLES ONLY OR FOR A PASTA
SALAD. HOWEVER, REMEMBER THAT FOR PASTA YOU NEED
QUITE A BIT OF DRESSING.

Combine all the ingredients and mix well.

YIELD: 1 ¹/₃ CUPS

1   cup salad oil (I prefer
    half olive oil, half
    salad oil)

¹/₃ cup red wine vinegar

1   tablespoon honey

1   tablespoon sweet rel-
    ish

    salt and pepper, to
    taste

Yogurt Cardamom Dressing

❖　❖　❖

**UNUSUAL FLAVOR. SERVE WITH A FRUITED CHICKEN OR
TURKEY SALAD.**

$^1/_2$ cup plain nonfat yogurt	Place all the ingredients in a processor or blender and blend well.
$^1/_3$ teaspoon ground cardamom	
1 tablespoon honey	YIELD: $^3/_4$ CUP
1 tablespoon balsamic vinegar or red wine vinegar	
$^1/_2$ teaspoon salt	
1 teaspoon pepper	

Classic Greek Dressing

❖　❖　❖

Fresh lemon juice is the secret of a good Greek dressing.

Blend the first seven ingredients in your blender or food processor and store in the refrigerator. When serving over your greens, add the cheese.

2 to 3 cloves fresh garlic

$^1/_8$　cup white wine vinegar

$^1/_4$　cup fresh lemon juice

$^3/_4$　cup extra-virgin olive oil

1　teaspoon salt

$^1/_8$　teaspoon white pepper

1　teaspoon dried Greek seasonings

　　crumbled feta cheese

Fish

Grandma Celia's Gefilte Fish

❖　❖　❖

THIS WAS GRANDMA CELIA'S RECIPE. THERE'S NOTHING LIKE
THE AROMA OF GEFILTE FISH COOKING. LIKE IT OR NOT,
IT IS VERY NOSTALGIC.

IF YOU LIVE IN A REGION WHERE THE FOLLOWING TYPES OF
FISH ARE NOT AVAILABLE, SUBSTITUTE AS BEST YOU CAN.
BE SURE TO ASK THE FISH MARKET FOR THE BONES,
IF AVAILABLE.

In a food processor, using the steel blade, combine the fish, egg, water, sugar, and salt and pepper. Be sure you process the fish well enough so that it is of a smooth consistency. Form into desired-size balls.

Line a stockpot with the bones and sliced onions and carrots, and fill with water as you would for a soup. Bring to a boil. Place the fish balls in the pot very carefully. Reduce to medium heat and cook for about 1¹/₂ hours. Remove pot from heat and allow to cool. Lift fish balls out of the pot very carefully.

Serve cold with red or white horseradish.

YIELD: **12 SERVINGS**

2	pounds whitefish
2	pounds trout
2	pounds pike
1	whole egg
1	6-ounce glass cold water (she used a Yahrzeit glass)
1	tablespoon sugar
	salt and pepper, to taste
	fish bones
	sliced onions and carrots

Baked Fish à la Turner

❖ ❖ ❖

I CONSIDERED MRS. TURNER ONE OF THE FINEST COOKS I
HAVE EVER KNOWN. THIS WAS SERVED AT MANY A SISTERHOOD
LUNCHEON AT OUR TEMPLE AND WAS ALWAYS ONE OF MY
FAVORITES. WOULD YOU BELIEVE,
MY FAMILY NEVER LIKED IT!

6 *fillets of your favorite fish, 1 inch thick*	Preheat oven to 350°F.
garlic powder	Grease a baking dish and place fish in it, skin side down.
touch of sugar	Sprinkle fish with the garlic powder, a touch of sugar, and the
Beau Monde seasoning	Beau Monde seasoning.
2 *medium onions, sliced*	Sauté or microwave the onions, celery, and carrots in the margarine or butter. Add the tomato soup, sour cream, salt and pepper, and the curry powder. Blend well.
4 to 5 *celery stalks, chopped*	
4 to 6 *carrots, sliced*	Pour the vegetable sauce over the fish.
2 *tablespoons margarine or butter*	
1 *can tomato soup (undiluted)*	Bake for 1 hour, uncovered.
1 *cup sour cream*	YIELD: 6 SERVINGS
salt and pepper, to taste	
¹/₈ *teaspoon curry powder*	

Salmon Mousse

❖ ❖ ❖

THIS WAS ALWAYS A FAVORITE AT BRIDAL LUNCHEONS. I HAVE ALSO SERVED THIS AT MANY A BRUNCH.

Combine the salmon, green pepper, celery, onion, mayonnaise, and Worcestershire sauce and blend well. Set aside.

Heat the cream cheese in the tomato soup until thoroughly blended. Reheat gelatin for a few seconds and add to the cream cheese mixture. Blend well.

Add the soup mixture to the salmon and vegetables. Mix thoroughly. Season to taste.

Pour into a greased mold and allow to set for several hours. This can be made a day in advance.

Unmold and garnish.

This recipe adapts well to all the lower fat products.

YIELD: **12 TO 18** SERVINGS

2 14¾-ounce cans red or pink salmon

2 cups minced green pepper

2 cups diced celery

1 large sweet onion, diced

2 cups mayonnaise

½ teaspoon Worcestershire sauce

1 8-ounce package cream cheese

1 can cream of tomato soup, undiluted

4 tablespoons unflavored gelatin, dissolved in ½ cup hot water

   salt to taste

Gefilte Fish Mold with Horseradish

❖ ❖ ❖

A GREAT APPETIZER, FIRST COURSE, OR A BRUNCH OR
BUFFET ITEM.

1   6-ounce package
    lime Jell-O

2   cups boiling water

1   cup fish liquid

1   5-ounce jar white
    horseradish

    juice of ¹/₂ lemon

1¹/₂ 24-ounce jars gefilte
    fish, drained (save
    juice), cut into thick
    slices

Combine the gelatin with the boiling water and fish liquid. Stir until completely dissolved. Add horseradish and lemon juice to gelatin and blend. Pour some gelatin into a ring mold and chill until firm. Place the slices of fish vertically over the chilled gelatin, and pour the balance of the gelatin mixture over the fish. Chill until very firm.

Unmold and garnish.

YIELD: 12 SERVINGS

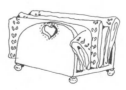

Lox

❖　❖　❖

SLICED ON A DIAGONAL, GARNISHED WITH CAPERS AND
THINLY SLICED SWEET ONIONS, SERVED ON SMALL SLICES OF
DARK PUMPERNICKEL—THIS IS A REAL DELICACY!

Mix together the kosher salt, the Spice Island Old Hickory Smoked Salt, and the sugar. Rub the fillet of salmon on both sides and place in a large glass dish. Cover tightly with foil and weight down with bricks, if available, and heavy cans.

Refrigerate for 4 days. At the end of the 4th day, pour off all liquid. Recover, weight down again, and return to the refrigerator for another 4 days. At the end of that time, pour off any liquid.

Wrap well and freeze. Cut partially frozen on a slight slant.

YIELD: 18 TO 20 SLICES

8　teaspoons kosher salt

1　tablespoon Spice Island Old Hickory Smoked Salt

2　tablespoons sugar

3　pounds center-cut fresh salmon fillet, skinned

Salmon Patties

❖ ❖ ❖

IF YOUR CHILDHOOD WAS LIKE MINE, YOU SURELY REMEMBER
SALMON PATTIES. THERE WERE NO RESTRICTIONS ON FRIED
FOODS IN THE OLD DAYS, SO WE WERE SERVED THESE
QUITE OFTEN. WE LOVED THEM.

1   14 ¾ -ounce can red
    salmon, drained (do
    not discard bones)

1   small white onion,
    grated

1   whole egg, well
    beaten

¹/₃   cup sour cream

¹/₃   cup seasoned bread
    crumbs

¹/₈   teaspoon white pep-
    per

¹/₄   teaspoon curry pow-
    der

1   tablespoon fresh
    lemon juice

    extra seasoned bread
    crumbs

    peanut oil

Mix all the ingredients together, except the extra crumbs and
oil, mashing the bones carefully. They are very nutritious.

Make round balls of the mixture. Flatten slightly and roll in the
extra bread crumbs. Place in the hot oil and fry until crisp on
both sides.

YIELD: 6 PATTIES

Salmon Quiche

❖ ❖ ❖

FROM THE KITCHEN OF LOIS KURS. WHO SAID LOIS DIDN'T COOK? I OFTEN MAKE THIS FOR DINNER JUST FOR THE TWO OF US. FOR A BRUNCH, I DOUBLE THE RECIPE, USING A LARGER ROUND BAKING DISH.

Preheat oven to 350°F.

Beat eggs and milk together. Add to salmon and onions. Blend. Add seasonings.

Place in an oven proof 8-inch quiche dish. Cover with aluminum foil. Bake for 30 minutes. Uncover and continue baking until lightly brown.

Cut into wedges and serve.

YIELD: 4 SERVINGS

2   eggs

$^{1}/_{2}$ cup milk

1   14 $^{3}/_{4}$-ounce can red or pink salmon, flaked and boned

1   2.8-ounce can French-fried onion rings

    juice of 1 lemon

$^{1}/_{8}$ teaspoon pepper

$^{1}/_{2}$ teaspoon curry powder

    salt, to taste

Roasted Salmon

❖ ❖ ❖

THIS IS A NO-FAIL METHOD FOR COOKING SALMON.
BETTER THAN POACHING.

I HAVE COME TO SALSAS LATE IN LIFE AND LOVE THEM. THEY
ARE AVAILABLE IN ANY GOURMET FOOD STORE. FISH WITH
THE TERIYAKI SAUCE DEVELOPS A WONDERFUL SWEET-AND-
SOUR TASTE, WHEN REFRIGERATED.

*Whole fillets of
salmon, as thick as
possible, center cuts
preferred*

*Beau Monde season-
ing*

fresh lemon juice

*Yoshida Gourmet
Sauce or another
teriyaki marinade of
your choice*

or

*a pineapple or rasp-
berry salsa*

or

*a cucumber sauce, if
served cold (recipe
follows)*

Preheat oven to 450°F.

Place fish on a greased baking dish. Sprinkle lightly with Beau
Monde seasoning and a little fresh lemon juice. Bake for 18 to
20 minutes, depending upon thickness. Remove from oven and
serve with any of the sauces mentioned above.

YIELD: ¹/₂ POUND PER SERVING

Cucumber Sauce

❖   ❖   ❖

THIS IS DELICIOUS WITH COLD POACHED SALMON.

Place all the ingredients in a food processor. Blend with pulsing motion. Do not overprocess as mixture will become too watery.

This should be made in advance so that the ingredients blend well.

YIELD: 2 CUPS

1   large cucumber, halved and seeded, cut into chunks

¹/₂   cup mayonnaise (regular or low-fat)

¹/₂   cup sour cream (regular or low-fat)

¹/₂   teaspoon Dijon mustard

1   tablespoon fresh lemon juice

1   tablespoon chives or finely cut green onions

1   heaping teaspoon dill

Sweet-and-Sour Fish

❖   ❖   ❖

MANY YEARS AGO, MY DEAR FRIEND BELLA SMITH OBTAINED
THIS RECIPE FROM HER MOTHER-IN-LAW, JENNIE. IT TOOK ALL
DAY INASMUCH AS JENNIE HAD NOTHING WRITTEN DOWN.
BELLA WORKED WITH HER, WRITING AND CHANGING AS THEY
WENT ALONG. WHEN THEY WERE FINISHED, WE HAD AN
EXACT RECIPE FOR JENNIE'S SWEET-AND-SOUR PICKLED FISH.
THIS TOOK THE PLACE OF ALL THE OTHER RECIPES WE HAD
FOR SWEET OR PICKLED FISH. EVERYONE LOVED IT.
THANK YOU, BELLA!

9	cups water
3	cups white vinegar
3	teaspoons salt
1	tablespoon mixed pickling spices
3	cups sugar
	juice of 1 large lemon
5 to 6	pounds fish slices with bone in (you cannot use boned fish for boiling)
2	lemons, sliced very thin
2	medium onions, sliced

In a large stockpot, place everything except the fish, sliced lemons, and onions and bring to a boil. Cook gently for 20 minutes. Place slices of fish very carefully into hot liquid and cook for 30 minutes. Remove from heat and cool.

When cool, remove fish and place in a bowl. Strain the liquid. Cover fish with the slices of lemon and sliced onions. Pour strained liquid over everything. Refrigerate for several days before serving

YIELD: 10 TO 12 SERVINGS

Tuna Burgers

❖　❖　❖

ONE DAY MANDY CAME HOME FROM A FRIEND'S HOUSE WITH
THIS RECIPE. AS A YOUNGSTER, THIS WAS HIS FAVORITE
SANDWICH. I BELIEVE HE STILL MAKES THIS FOR HIS BOYS.

Slightly toast hamburger buns or English muffins. Combine the ingredients for the burgers and spread mixture on buns or muffins. Sprinkle with grated Cheddar cheese. Broil until cheese bubbles.

YIELD: 4 TO 6 SERVINGS

1　small can white alba-core tuna, water packed

1　tablespoon dried minced onion

2　heaping tablespoons mayonnaise

2　tablespoons grated Parmesan cheese

$1/8$　teaspoon dried dill

2　tablespoons white wine

$1/8$　teaspoon salt

　　hamburger buns or English muffins

　　Cheddar cheese

Tuna Salad

❖ ❖ ❖

"TOONEY" SALAD WAS ALWAYS A STAPLE IN OUR FAMILY.
WHEN YOU DIDN'T KNOW WHAT TO MAKE FOR LUNCH, OUT
CAME THE CANS OF TUNA. MOST OF MY GRANDCHILDREN
PREFERRED "JUST PLAIN TUNA," BUT THIS IS MY
VERSION OF AN OLD STANDARD.

2	6-ounce cans water-packed white tuna
4	stalks celery, finely diced
1	tablespoon fresh lemon juice
1	teaspoon dried dill weed
1/8	teaspoon white pepper
4	tablespoons mayonnaise
1	tablespoon plain yogurt
1	tablespoon grated parmesan cheese
1/2	cup roasted pine nuts (optional). Toast at about 250°F in your toaster oven. Stir occasionally. Watch carefully.

Drain the tuna and transfer to a large bowl. Combine all of the ingredients and blend well. Refrigerate, if possible, for at least 1 hour.

YIELD: 6 SERVINGS

Poultry

Oriental Stir-Fry Chicken

❖ ❖ ❖

I DO NOT USE ANY OIL FOR FRYING! THIS MAKES A
BEAUTIFUL PRESENTATION AND THE TASTE IS MARVELOUS.

In a small mixing bowl, combine the chicken soup, cornstarch, and ¼ cup of the Yoshida sauce. Set aside.

Combine the chicken with crushed garlic, and ginger. Sauté chicken in ¼ cup of Yoshida sauce. When tender, set aside. In the same pan, add ¼ cup additional sauce and sauté the vegetables just until crisp. Combine chicken and vegetables. Pour the chicken soup mixture over the chicken and vegetables and heat until sauce is thickened. Do not allow the vegetables to become too soft.

Sprinkle a tablespoon of sesame oil over the ingredients and garnish with some toasted almonds or sesame seeds.

Serve with steamed rice.

YIELD: **4 SERVINGS**

³/₄ cup clear chicken soup (canned is okay)

2 tablespoons corn-starch

³/₄ cup Yoshida Gourmet Sauce (or any good teriyaki marinade)

4 large chicken breasts, cut into pieces, or 16 chicken tenders, cut into thirds.

2 garlic cloves, crushed

¹/₂ teaspoon ground ginger

8 Roma tomatoes, halved or quartered, depending upon size

1 cup broccoli florets

8 large white mush-rooms, sliced

4 small zucchini, sliced rather thick

1 can sliced water chestnuts

sesame oil

toasted almonds or toasted sesame seeds

Crispy Barbecued Chicken

❖   ❖   ❖

SURPRISE FLAVOR AND OH, SO EASY. I MAKE THIS ALL THE TIME.

6   chicken breasts, bone-
     less and skinless

¹/₂   cup barbecue sauce

2   cups crushed herb-
     seasoned stuffing

     olive oil

Preheat oven to 375°F.

Dip chicken breasts into barbecue sauce. Coat with crushed stuffing.

Place chicken on a greased baking pan. Brush lightly with a little olive oil and any remaining barbecue sauce.

Bake for 45 minutes.

YIELD: 6 SERVINGS

Lemon Artichoke Chicken

❖　❖　❖

EASY TO MAKE AND WONDERFUL FOR GUESTS. THIS FREEZES
WELL. DEFROST AND HEAT IN A CONVENTIONAL OVEN AT
325°F FOR 30 MINUTES OR MICROWAVE ON HIGH
FOR 3 TO 5 MINUTES.

Grease a large pan generously with olive oil or with an olive oil spray.

Place seasoned stuffing mix and chicken breasts in a plastic bag and shake to coat lightly.

Preheat oven to 450°F. Place in greased pan, sprinkle with paprika, and bake for 15 minutes. Turn and bake another 15 minutes.

Remove to an ovenproof serving dish.

Toss mushrooms and artichokes over the chicken.

Combine lemon juice and wine and pour over the chicken.

At this point, this recipe can be frozen. Cover first with plastic wrap and then aluminum foil.

If not freezing, cover with aluminum foil and bake at 350°F for 30 minutes.

Baste before serving.

YIELD: **12** SERVINGS

seasoned stuffing mix, crushed in a food processor and mixed with a little Wondra or regular flour

12　boneless chicken breasts (if too thick, pound slightly)

paprika

1　pound fresh mushrooms, sliced

12　marinated artichoke hearts, drained

³/₄　cup fresh lemon juice

1　cup white wine such as Champagne, white Zinfandel, or a Chardonnay

Marsha's Pizza Chicken

❖   ❖   ❖

JUST SERVE OVER ANGEL HAIR OR LINGUINE PASTA.
FABULOUS. FROM THE KITCHEN OF MY DAUGHTER,
MARSHA PATINKIN.

*chicken breasts,
thighs and legs (bone
in)*

salt and pepper

oregano

garlic powder

diced green pepper

sliced mushrooms

chopped onions

pizza sauce

*grated Parmesan
cheese*

Preheat oven to 375°F.

Season the chicken well with salt, pepper, oregano, and garlic powder. Sprinkle generously with diced green pepper, mushrooms, and chopped onions. Cover with a thick pizza sauce and smother with grated parmesan cheese.

Bake for 1 hour.

Greek Chicken

❖ ❖ ❖

ONE OF MY FAVORITES! IF YOU LIKE GARLIC AND LEMON,
THIS IS A REAL WINNER.

You may use legs, thighs, and breasts (bone in), whichever you prefer.

Season chicken well with a good amount of minced fresh garlic, pepper, Lawry's seasoned salt, oregano. Brush with fresh lemon juice.

Sprinkle with mild paprika.

Place in a baking dish and bake at 400°F for 1 hour, turning twice.

When serving, skim the gravy, pour over the chicken, and enjoy the wonderful lemon flavor.

Glazed Cornish Hens

❖ ❖ ❖

THESE MAKE A BEAUTIFUL PRESENTATION SERVED WITH A
RICE OR COUSCOUS DISH AND A GREEN VEGETABLE. I HAVE
FOUND THAT SERVING A WHOLE CORNISH HEN CAN BE VERY
MESSY; THEREFORE, I ALWAYS CUT THEM IN HALF. IF YOU
USE A VERY SHARP KNIFE, THIS IS EASILY ACCOMPLISHED.

Cornish hens, split in half

garlic powder

ground ginger

salt

a gourmet teriyaki sauce

or

orange marmalade combined with a light soy sauce (to taste)

Preheat oven to 350°F.

Place the hens in a roasting pan and season them well on both sides with the garlic powder, ginger, and salt. Brush them on both sides with the teriyaki sauce or the orange marmalade and soy sauce. Roast them for 1¹/₂ hours, basting frequently. They will be beautifully glazed if basted often.

Grilled Turkey Breast

❖ ❖ ❖

THIS RECIPE HAS RECEIVED NOTHING BUT RAVES. MANDY
HAS PEOPLE CALLING ME FROM ALL OVER THE COUNTRY.
THANK YOU, ROBIN PATINKIN.

Combine all the ingredients for the marinade in a blender or food processor.

Place the marinade and the turkey breast in a large zippered freezer bag. Marinate for 6 to 12 hours, no more.

For grilling: Cook over medium heat for 20 to 25 minutes on each side, basting frequently. Remove from grill and allow to set for 20 to 25 minutes. Slice as you would a london broil.

For roasting: Place in roasting pan and baste well with marinade. Cover tightly and roast in a 350°F oven for 1½ hours. Uncover, baste well, and return to oven for about 15 minutes. Remove from oven and proceed as above.

YIELD: 12 SERVINGS

1   boned turkey breast,
    split (this will give
    you two tenderloins)

MARINADE:

2   large shallots, minced

½   cup orange juice

3   tablespoons olive oil

1   tablespoon fresh rose-
    mary, or 2 teaspoons
    dried

2   tablespoons balsamic
    vinegar

1   tablespoon honey

1   teaspoon salt

⅛   teaspoon dried
    crushed red pepper

Oven-Roasted Turkey

❖   ❖   ❖

I KNOW THERE ARE SEVERAL SCHOOLS OF THOUGHT AS TO HOW A BIRD SHOULD BE ROASTED. I HAVE ALWAYS OPTED FOR "BREAST DOWN."

Wash and clean the inside of the bird. Season it well with garlic, poultry seasoning, salt, and pepper. Place a whole onion, several ribs of celery, and a sweet apple in the cavity of the bird.

Place bird, *breast down,* in roasting pan and tent loosely with aluminum foil. Follow the timetable for roasting below. Remove foil the last half hour of roasting and allow to brown.

Remove from oven, cover lightly with the foil, and allow to stand for at least 10 minutes before carving. This allows the juices to settle.

TIMETABLE:

10 to 12 lbs.	unstuffed	350°F	$2^1/4$ hours
	stuffed	325°F	$3^1/2$ hours
14 to 20 lbs.	unstuffed	325°F	3 hours
	stuffed	300°F	$4^1/2$ to $5^1/2$ hours
20 to 25 lbs.	unstuffed	325°F	$3^3/4$ hours
	stuffed	275°–300°F	5 to $6^1/2$ hours

Grandma Doralee's Turkey Stuffing

❖   ❖   ❖

THIS IS A NEVER-FAIL RECIPE. JUST ASK MANDY.

In a very deep skillet, heat the butter or margarine.

Pour the chicken stock over the stuffing mix and cereal to moisten well. For a looser stuffing, use more chicken stock.

Use a food processor to prepare the vegetables and apricots. As they are of different textures, I suggest doing one at a time; no need to wash the processor in between, just transfer to melting butter or margarine in frying pan and proceed to the next item.

Sauté the mushrooms, onions, and celery and add to the stuffing mix. Beat the eggs lightly and blend into the stuffing mixture. If using apricots, add them at this point. Add poultry seasoning, sage, salt, pepper, and pine nuts. Adjust seasonings to taste.

Stuff the bird and roast at once (see preceding recipe), or refrigerate.

Any extra stuffing can be baked in a casserole at 325°F; covered for the first half hour, and then uncovered until a crust forms.

FOR A 14- TO 16-
POUND TURKEY:

¹/₂ pound butter or margarine

2 to 3 cups chicken stock (canned or fresh)

1   large package seasoned stuffing mix

1   cup Grape Nuts cereal

1   pound fresh mushrooms, sliced

3   large onions, diced

4   celery ribs, sliced

4   eggs

1   cup diced dried apricots (optional)

1   teaspoon poultry seasoning

1   teaspoon sage

salt and pepper, to taste

¹/₂ cup toasted pine nuts

Turkey Gravy

❖ ❖ ❖

A NEVER-FAIL RECIPE.

Giblets from turkey
(neck, liver, and giz-
zard)

2 carrots, cut into
chunks

3 celery ribs, cut into
large pieces

1 large onion, cut into
chunks

1 bay leaf

1/4 teaspoon poultry seasoning

1/4 teaspoon salt

1/8 teaspoon white pep-
per

2 tablespoons corn-
starch

1/3 cup cold water

Place the giblets, carrots, celery, onion, bay leaf, and seasonings in a large saucepan with some water, and boil as you would a soup stock. Cook for about 1 hour.

Remove vegetables and bay leaf and discard. Remove giblets; cut into small pieces and set aside. Using a gravy separator, eliminate as much fat as you can. Return the giblets, if you desire, to the stock and set aside.

When the turkey is done, try to remove the fat from the drippings in the pan and add the drippings to the stock; bring to a boil. Dissolve the cornstarch in the cold water and add to the hot stock. Stir until it thickens slightly.

Sweet-and-Sour Sauce for Poultry

❖　❖　❖

THIS SAUCE WAS AN OLD FAMILY FAVORITE, USED BY MYSELF AND AUNTIES LILLIAN, IDA, AND JUNE.

Blend well. Spread over chicken, capon, or turkey and bake.

Can be stored in refrigerator for several weeks.

YIELD: 1 1/2 CUPS

1　10-ounce bottle sweet-and-sour sauce

1/4　cup white wine

1/4　cup ketchup

Russian Dressing Marinade and Sauce

❖　❖　❖

AN OLD, OLD RECIPE, BUT OH, SO GOOD!

1　envelope onion soup mix

1　16-ounce can whole cranberries sauce

1　8-ounce bottle Russian dressing

Combine all the ingredients and use as a marinade and sauce for chicken. Spread over the chicken and bake as usual, basting once in a while.

YIELD: **2 TO 3 CUPS**

Meat

Brisket 1

❖ ❖ ❖

THIS, OF COURSE, IS TRADITIONAL HOLIDAY FARE AND WAS
ALWAYS A FAMILY FAVORITE. I NEVER GET ENOUGH. HOT OR
COLD, IT'S WONDERFUL. THE DELICATESSENS EVERYWHERE
COULD TAKE NOTE.

Preheat oven to 325°F.

Season brisket well with Lawry's seasoning. Sprinkle brisket
with the brown sugar and the cider vinegar. Frost with the chili
sauce, and with the back of a large spoon, rub everything into
the meat.

Bake uncovered until semi-tender. Cover and roast until done.
In cooking a brisket, the total time could vary from 1¹/₂ to 3
hours. You must test from time to time.

Remove meat from gravy and cool. Allow gravy to cool. Skim
fat. Add water to dilute as gravy will be a little strong. Taste.

Slice the brisket and place in an ovenproof casserole. Cover
with gravy and seal tightly with aluminum foil. Heat and serve.

This may be made in advance and frozen. Slice, add gravy,
cover with plastic wrap, and then aluminum foil.

When ready to serve, remove plastic wrap, cover again with
aluminum foil, and heat in conventional oven at 325°F.

YIELD: 10 TO 12 SERVINGS

1   brisket of beef (fat side up)

    Lawry's seasoned salt

¹/₂ cup brown sugar

2   tablespoons cider vinegar

1   cup chili sauce

Brisket 2

❖ ❖ ❖

THIS IS ANOTHER VERSION OF A TRADITIONAL FAVORITE. THE
APRICOTS, ONIONS, AND WINE GIVE THIS BRISKET A SUPERB
FLAVOR. A REAL WINNER!

1	brisket of beef (fat side up)
	Lawry's seasoned salt
1/4	cup brown sugar
1/2	cup semi-dry red wine
1/2	cup chili sauce
2	large onions, chopped
1	cup chopped dried apricots

Preheat oven to 325 F.

Season brisket well with Lawry's seasoning. Sprinkle brisket
with the brown sugar and red wine. Frost with the chili sauce,
and with the back of a large spoon, rub everything into the meat.
Place in baking pan and add chopped onions and dried apricots.

Bake uncovered until semi-tender. Cover and roast until done.
In cooking a brisket, the total time could vary from 1 1/2 to 3
hours. You must test from time to time.

Remove meat from gravy and cool. Allow gravy to cool. Skim
fat. Add water to dilute as gravy will be a little strong. Taste.

Slice the brisket and place in an ovenproof casserole. Cover
with gravy and seal tightly with aluminum foil. Heat and serve.

This may be made in advance and frozen. Slice, add gravy,
cover with plastic wrap, and then aluminum foil.

When ready to serve, remove plastic wrap, cover again with
aluminum foil, and heat in conventional oven at 325°F.

YIELD: 10 TO 12 SERVINGS

Roast Corned Beef Brisket

❖   ❖   ❖

VERY DIFFERENT FROM MY OTHER BRISKET RECIPES. THIS IS
MARVELOUS—HOT OR COLD. MAKES WONDERFUL
SANDWICHES. IF SERVING AS A MAIN COURSE, MAKE MY
CANDIED SWEET POTATOES TO GO ALONG.

In a large stockpot, boil the brisket with the bay leaves and garlic, in just enough water to cover the meat.

While brisket is cooking, combine juice or 7-UP, mustard, and brown sugar.

When meat is almost tender, remove from pot and allow to cool. Pierce with some whole cloves and spread the sauce over the top of the brisket. Roast in a 300°F oven for about an hour, until it's completely tender and nicely glazed.

YIELD: 10 TO 12 SERVINGS

1   corned beef brisket

3   whole bay leaves

3   whole garlic cloves

1   cup pineapple juice or
    7-UP

$^1/_3$ cup Dijon mustard

2   tablespoons dark
    brown sugar

    whole cloves

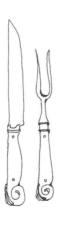

Roasted Filet Mignon (Whole Tenderloin of Beef)

❖   ❖   ❖

I LOVE SERVING THIS. IT IS VERY VERSATILE. I HAVE USED IT AS THE MAIN ENTRÉE, AS PART OF A BUFFET SUPPER, OR FOR SMALL BEEF SANDWICHES, ALSO PART OF A BUFFET SUPPER. SLICE IT THICK, SLICE IT THIN. SERVE IT HOT, SERVE IT COLD. IT IS ALWAYS WONDERFUL.

1 whole beef tenderloin (trimmed)	Preheat oven to 450°F.
garlic powder	Season the beef on both sides with the garlic powder, seasoned salt, and caraway seed. Frost with your favorite chili sauce and add a little water to the pan.
Lawry's seasoned salt	
caraway seed	
chili sauce	

Bake for 25 minutes for rare, 35 minutes for medium, 45 minutes for well done. Time may vary—test.

If more gravy is needed, add a little more water to the pan.

Allow meat to stand for about 10 minutes before slicing. Slice to desired thickness.

Marinated Flank Steak

❖   ❖   ❖

THE FLAVOR OF A FLANK STEAK IS WONDERFUL. IT IS
DELICIOUS SERVED HOT, AND WONDERFUL AS COLD
LEFTOVERS FOR SANDWICHES.

Unfold flank steak. Score on each side. Rub both sides with chopped garlic and brush amply with the teriyaki sauce.

Marinate in the refrigerator for several hours. When ready to serve, brush with the marinade; if necessary, add more sauce, and broil for about 8 minutes on each side. If too rare, return to broiler until done.

Slice on the diagonal and serve with the natural gravy.

Note: As a marinade, you can substitute an Italian salad dressing, but I prefer the teriyaki.

1   *flank steak*

2 to 3 *cloves fresh garlic, chopped*

teriyaki sauce

Marinated Rack of Lamb

❖　❖　❖

THIS IS A GOURMET DELIGHT! SERVE WITH A RICE OR
COUSCOUS DISH. THE MARINADE HAS AN UNUSUAL FLAVOR.

rack or racks of lamb
(trimmed)

Red Pepper Marinade
(see following recipe)

Coat lamb with the marinade. Cover and refrigerate for at least
4 hours, or overnight.

Preheat oven to 475°F.

Place rack or racks, bone side down, in a greased roasting pan.

Roast for 20 minutes.

Reduce oven temperature to 400°F.

Reverse rack or racks of lamb; place fat side down, and return
to oven for 20 minutes. This should be medium rare.

If using a meat thermometer, insert in thickest part of rack, and
continue cooking until temperature of 140°F is reached for
medium rare.

Red Pepper Marinade

❖ ❖ ❖

WONDERFUL FLAVOR! THIS CAN BE USED FOR RACK OF LAMB,
BUTTERFLIED LEG OF LAMB, TURKEY BREAST, OR CHICKEN—
IN THE OVEN OR ON THE GRILL.

Combine all the ingredients in a food processor or blender and blend just until mixture is of a chopped consistency. Do not purée. Refrigerate until ready to use.

4 marinated red pepper halves

2 tablespoons port wine

2 tablespoons honey

1 1/2 tablespoons dry mustard

1/2 cup Dijon mustard

1 teaspoon minced fresh or dried rosemary

Mandy and Kathryn's Butterflied Leg of Lamb

❖ ❖ ❖

THIS IS A REAL WINNER! WHO SAYS YOU CAN'T LEARN FROM YOUR CHILDREN? THIS IS ESPECIALLY WONDERFUL AROUND THE HOLIDAYS. THERE IS ABSOLUTELY NOTHING THAT CAN TAKE ITS PLACE.

1　butterflied leg of lamb (your local butcher will do this for you)

6 to 8 fresh garlic cloves, crushed (more if you like garlic)

$^{1}/_{2}$　cup tamari or soy sauce

$^{1}/_{2}$　cup honey

Pierce the leg of lamb on both sides and cover with the crushed garlic. Combine the tamari or soy sauce with the honey and pour over the leg of lamb. Marinate overnight, if possible.

When ready, broil 12 to 15 minutes on each side. Slice on a slight diagonal as you would a London broil.

YIELD: 12 SERVINGS

Hamburger on Russian Rye

❖ ❖ ❖

WHEN MY CHILDREN WERE SMALL, I SERVED THIS ON
MINIATURE HAMBURGER BUNS. THIS WAS ALWAYS A
WINNER AT BIRTHDAY PARTIES. AS THEY MATURED, WE
GRADUATED TO THE LARGE SLICES OF RUSSIAN RYE.
THE ADULTS WERE JUST AS PLEASED.

I RECENTLY SERVED THESE TO A GROUP OF FRIENDS AND IT
WAS VERY NOSTALGIC FOR ALL OF US.

Combine the sirloin, onion soup mix, and chili sauce. Spread
the ground meat mixture over each slice of bread, bringing the
meat over the edge as the meat will shrink. Frost with chili
sauce or ketchup.

Place under broiler about 5 inches from heat. Broil about 5 minutes, or until top is glazed. Test for rare, medium, or well done.

YIELD: 6 TO 8 SERVINGS

2 pounds ground sir-
   loin

1 envelope dried onion
   soup mix

$^1/_2$ cup chili sauce

   slices of Russian rye
   bread, slightly toasted

   chili sauce or ketchup

Barbecued Hamburger (Sloppy Joes)

❖ ❖ ❖

BRINGS BACK MEMORIES OF WHEN MY CHILDREN WERE
YOUNG. WHAT MOTHER DIDN'T SERVE HER KIDS
SLOPPY JOES? I LOVED THEM, TOO.

2	pounds ground meat
1	large onion, finely chopped
1	tablespoon olive oil
1	12-ounce bottle chili sauce (rinse out bottle with water and include)
1/4	teaspoon Tabasco sauce
1/4	teaspoon paprika
1/2	teaspoon chili powder
2	teaspoons Worcestershire sauce
2	teaspoons salt
1/2	teaspoon black pepper
	toasted hamburger buns

Brown the ground meat and chopped onion in the olive oil. Add the balance of the ingredients. Bring to a boil and reduce to a slow simmer for about 45 minutes.

Serve on toasted hamburger buns.

YIELD: 6 SERVINGS

Prune Tzimmes

❖ ❖ ❖

THIS WAS NEVER THE MAIN COURSE, BUT MY MOTHER,
GRANDMA IDA, ALWAYS MADE IT, AND I ALWAYS LOVED IT.
WHY DO PEOPLE SHY AWAY FROM PRUNES? TRY IT,
YOU MAY LIKE IT!

In a large pot, place the apple juice, orange juice, and lemon juice. Add the salt and sugar, cardamom, and peppercorns. Add the ¹/₂ cup water. Bring to a boil, and place the meat in the sauce. Cook until almost tender; add the prunes and potatoes and continue cooking for at least 1 hour on low heat. Baste every so often.

For a stronger sweet-and-sour flavor, adjust with salt and lemon juice, just a little at a time.

YIELD: 6 TO 8 SERVINGS

12 ounces frozen apple juice (undiluted)

4 ounces frozen orange juice (undiluted)

¹/₄ cup fresh lemon juice

2 teaspoons salt

¹/₂ cup sugar, or 2 teaspoons Sweet 'n Low

¹/₄ teaspoon cardamom

8 whole black peppercorns

¹/₂ cup water

2 pounds sirloin steak or filet mignon, cut into small chunks

1 pound medium-size prunes, pitted

4 large sweet potatoes, cut into chunks

Broiled or Grilled Veal Chops

❖　❖　❖

**ABSOLUTELY SUPERB! COMPANY FARE.
IF YOU LIKE VEAL, THIS IS IT.**

veal chops, about 1¹/₂ inches thick

garlic powder

Beau Monde seasoning

soy sauce or teriyaki sauce

Season the chops well with the garlic powder and Beau Monde seasoning. Prick chops on both sides and marinate in the soy or teriyaki sauce in the refrigerator for several hours. Turn every so often.

Remove chops to broiling pan or grill and broil or cook for 6 to 8 minutes on each side.

Hot Dogs and Baked Beans

❖　❖　❖

THIS WAS ALWAYS A FAVORITE AT OUR TEMPLE PARTIES
GIVEN FOR THE CHILDREN. MANDY REMEMBERS IT WELL AND
REQUESTED THAT IT BE INCLUDED.

TO THIS DAY, WHENEVER IT IS SERVED, IT IS A WHOPPING
SUCCESS. WHO SAID WE SHOULDN'T EAT HOT DOGS?

Combine all the ingredients in a large saucepan and simmer for
about 45 minutes.

YIELD: 6 TO 8 SERVINGS

2　1-pound cans vegetar-
　ian baked beans

6 to 8 kosher-style hot
　dogs, cut into chunks

1　large can pineapple
　chunks (drained well)

$^{1}/_{2}$　cup chili sauce

2　tablespoons prepared
　mustard

Pasta and Rice Dishes

Linguine Limone with Salmon

❖   ❖   ❖

THE BUTTERY-LEMONY FLAVOR OF THIS DISH IS BOUND TO
PLEASE MOST PALATES. THIS IS REALLY COMPANY FARE,
BUT I PREPARE IT ALL THE TIME JUST FOR MY
HUSBAND AND MYSELF.

Marinate the salmon in 2 tablespoons of the soy sauce, 1/4 cup of the lemon juice, and the seasoning for at least 1 hour.

Prepare the pasta just before you sauté the salmon. Drain and set aside.

In a very large skillet or wok, melt the butter, add the remaining soy sauce, salmon in the marinade, and mushrooms and sauté quickly.

Move the salmon and mushrooms to one side of the pan; add the hot pasta to the sauce, add the second 1/4 cup of lemon juice, and the pepper. Toss carefully; incorporate the salmon and mushrooms gently. Should you feel you need a little more lemon juice or soy sauce, by all means go for it.

Add the green onions, toss lightly, garnish with the toasted pine nuts, and serve immediately.

YIELD: 2 SERVINGS

3/4   pound salmon fillet, skinned and boned, cut in half length- wise, and sliced into 1/4-inch pieces

4   tablespoons light soy sauce

1/2   cup fresh lemon juice

Beau Monde season- ing

1/3   pound linguine, cooked according to directions on package

4   tablespoons butter or margarine

4   large white mush- rooms, sliced

1/4   teaspoon white pep- per

1/3   cup finely cut green onions

1/2   cup toasted pine nuts

Orzo à la Me

❖ ❖ ❖

ORZO IS A PASTA THAT LOOKS LIKE LARGE GRAINS OF RICE.
IT IS THE ITALIAN VERSION OF OUR FARFEL, AND A GREAT
ALTERNATIVE TO POTATOES OR RICE.

12 ounces fresh mush-
rooms, sliced

1 4-ounce jar sliced
pimiento

1 large onion, diced

4 tablespoons butter

1 package orzo pasta,
prepared according
to directions on pack-
age

1/4 teaspoon garlic
powder

1/2 teaspoon curry
powder

1/8 teaspoon white
pepper

1/4 teaspoon Lawry's
seasoned salt

olive oil

Grease a frying pan with olive oil and sauté the mushrooms, pimiento, and the onions until onions are glassy. Remove from stove and add the butter.

Combine the cooked orzo with the hot vegetable mixture and add all the seasonings. Blend well.

This can be made ahead of time. Place in a microwaveable casserole and heat when ready to serve.

YIELD: 6 TO 8 SERVINGS

Pesto Sauce

❖   ❖   ❖

PESTO IS MY FAVORITE PASTA SAUCE, ESPECIALLY WHEN I THROW IN SOME COOKED SHRIMP.

Place all the ingredients in a food processor and blend well. Season with extra salt, if necessary.

When using with cooked pasta, as you drain the pasta, save some of the cooking liquid and add it to the pasta and pesto to give a creamier consistency.

This pesto can be stored, covered, in the refrigerator for a week, or in the freezer for up to 2 months.

YIELD: ABOUT 1 CUP

2   *fresh garlic cloves*

2¹/₂ *cups fresh basil leaves*

¹/₂ *cup grated Parmesan cheese*

4   *tablespoons extra-virgin olive oil*

1   *teaspoon salt*

1 to 2 *tablespoons water (enough to make a smooth paste)*

¹/₃ *cup pine nuts or walnuts*

Rice and Noodles

❖   ❖   ❖

THIS IS MY VERSION OF A POPULAR DISH. IT IS A
WONDERFUL ACCOMPANIMENT TO MEAT OR POULTRY.

1/4   pound butter

8   ounces very fine noodles

1   cup sliced or slivered blanched almonds

12   ounces sliced fresh mushrooms

2   cups raw long-grain rice

1   14-ounce can defatted chicken broth

1   14-ounce can French onion soup (undiluted)

1   can sliced water chestnuts

Melt 6 tablespoons of the butter in a large frying pan and brown the noodles and almonds. Remove from pan and set aside.

In the same pan, heat remaining butter and sauté the fresh mushrooms. Combine the mushrooms with the noodles and almonds. Add the rice and both soups. Cover and simmer for about 25 minutes. When finished, add the water chestnuts.

This can be made in advance and reheated in the microwave.

YIELD: 6 TO 8 SERVINGS

Spinach Noodle Soufflé

❖   ❖   ❖

THIS IS NOT EXACTLY IN KEEPING WITH TODAY'S LOW-FAT
MENUS, BUT IT IS SOOOO GOOD. FROM THE KITCHEN
OF VIVIAN GILL.

Preheat oven to 350°F.

Prepare noodles according to directions on package.

Blend all the ingredients well.

Place in a well-greased 2-quart oblong casserole.

Bake for 45 to 60 minutes. Allow to set for a few minutes before
serving.

YIELD: 6 SERVINGS

16   ounces fine or medium noodles

1   10 ³/₄-ounce can cream of mushroom soup, undiluted

1   cup shredded Cheddar cheese

2   packages Stouffer's Spinach Soufflé, defrosted

Cantonese Fried Rice

❖   ❖   ❖

THIS EVOKES MANY A MEMORY. I ALWAYS SERVED THIS WITH
ROAST BEEF, WHEN EVERYONE ATE ROAST BEEF. OF COURSE,
ALWAYS WITH ORIENTAL DISHES!

¹/₄ cup peanut oil

*4   slightly beaten eggs,
      or 1 cup egg substitute*

¹/₄ teaspoon pepper

*¹/₂ cup finely chopped
      green onions*

*3   tablespoons soy sauce
      (more or less to taste)*

*1   cup cooked long-
      grain rice*

Place the peanut oil in a large skillet. When very hot, add the slightly beaten eggs and fry for 2 or 3 minutes, breaking the eggs into small pieces as they cook. Add the balance of the ingredients and cook over moderate heat for about 5 minutes.

Adjust seasonings.

This may be made in advance and reheated in the microwave.

YIELD: **4 TO 6 SERVINGS**

Spinach Lasagne

❖   ❖   ❖

A FAST AND DELICIOUS WAY TO MAKE LASAGNE. FROM THE KITCHEN OF MY DEAR FRIEND, RUTH KANTER.

Preheat oven to 350°F.

Combine the ricotta cheese, egg, 1 cup of the mozzarella cheese, spinach, salt, oregano, and pepper.

In a greased 9 × 13-inch pan, layer 1 cup of the sauce, 3 uncooked noodles, and half of the cheese mixture. Repeat. Top with remaining noodles and sauce. Sprinkle with remaining (1 cup) mozzarella cheese. Pour the water around the inside edges of pan. Cover tightly with foil and bake for 1 hour and 15 minutes.

Remove from oven and let stand 15 minutes before serving.

YIELD: SERVES 6

1   pound ricotta cheese

1   egg

2   cups shredded mozzarella cheese

1   10-ounce package frozen chopped spinach, defrosted and drained

1   teaspoon salt

1   teaspoon oregano

$^1/_8$ teaspoon pepper

4   cups (32 ounces) spaghetti sauce

9   lasagna noodles, uncooked

1   cup water

Old-Fashioned Baked Spaghetti

❖ ❖ ❖

THIS WAS ALWAYS A FAVORITE OF MINE AND BRINGS BACK
MANY A MEMORY. MY MOTHER ALWAYS SERVED THIS WITH
SALMON PATTIES. TRY THIS WITH MY SALMON QUICHE.

1	pound spaghetti (I do not recommend angel hair pasta)
1	10 ³/₄-ounce can cream of tomato soup, undiluted
1	28- to 30-ounce can chopped plum tomatoes, or the equivalent of fresh
4	large garlic cloves, minced
¹/₄	cup chopped parsley
¹/₂	teaspoon fennel seed
1	teaspoon ground coriander
2	tablespoons dried basil leaves, crushed
1	tablespoon oregano
2	tablespoons dried minced onion
1	8-ounce can sliced mushrooms

Preheat oven to 350°F.

Cook the spaghetti for just a few minutes. Drain and set aside.

Combine the balance of the ingredients. Blend well. Add to the cooked spaghetti and pour into a greased casserole.

Bake, uncovered, for 1 hour.

YIELD: 6 TO 8 SERVINGS

Spaghetti Sauce with Meat

❖ ❖ ❖

NOTHING BETTER THAN A HEARTY PLATE OF SPAGHETTI AND
MEAT SAUCE, GARLIC BREAD, AND A GREEN SALAD.
FOR A PASTA PRIMAVERA, OMIT THE MEAT OR TURKEY.
MAKE THE SAUCE, AND DURING THE LAST 5 MINUTES
OF COOKING, ADD VEGETABLES OF YOUR CHOICE.

In a large skillet or stockpot, heat the olive oil and brown the ground beef or turkey. When brown, add the balance of ingredients, except the baking soda and vermouth. Mix well and simmer for 1 hour. During the last few minutes, add the baking soda. This helps neutralize the acid of the tomatoes. Mix well and continue to simmer for about 10 minutes. If using vermouth, add to sauce after removing from heat.

YIELD: 6 TO 8 SERVINGS

1/4	cup olive oil
2	pounds ground beef or ground turkey
1	28- to 30-ounce can plum tomatoes, cut into chunks
4	large fresh tomatoes, peeled and cut into chunks
12	large sun-dried tomato halves
4	large garlic cloves, minced
2	tablespoons minced fresh onion
1	teaspoon ground coriander
2	tablespoons dried basil
1	tablespoon oregano
12	ounces fresh mushrooms, sliced
1/4	teaspoon baking soda
1/4	cup sweet vermouth (optional)

Cellophane Noodles (Saifun)

❖ ❖ ❖

YOUR LOCAL SUPERMARKET MAY HAVE THESE. IF NOT,
THEY CAN BE PURCHASED AT ANY ASIAN FOOD STORE.
THEY SHOULD BE MADE OF BEAN OR YAM, NOT RICE.
THEY ARE A WONDERFUL ADDITION TO AN ORIENTAL
CHICKEN SALAD
(SEE PAGE 58).

In a 4- to 6-quart pan, bring 2 quarts of water to a boil. Add noodles and return to a boiling point, stirring just once.

Remove from heat and allow to stand until tender to the bite, 10 to 15 minutes.

Pour into a colander and, with scissors, snip noodles to desired length. Drain well.

Couscous

❖ ❖ ❖

COUSCOUS IS A GRAIN-LIKE PASTA. I NEVER MADE THIS WHEN
MY CHILDREN WERE YOUNG, BUT I HAVE COME TO ENJOY IT
AS MUCH AS ANY RICE DISH. IT IS WONDERFUL WITH
CHICKEN, LAMB, OR BEEF, AND IT IS A WONDERFUL
SUBSTITUTION FOR RICE DISHES.

Add the chicken soup powder and butter to the boiling water.
Blend. Add the couscous, herbs, and sun-dried tomatoes. Cover
and remove from heat. Allow to stand for 7 minutes. Fluff with
a fork.

Optional: You can add canned or fresh sautéed mushrooms or
frozen petite peas or shredded carrots.

2	cups boiling water
1	tablespoon instant chicken soup powder
1	tablespoon butter
8	ounces couscous
	herbs and spices of choice
8	sun-dried tomatoes, cut into small pieces

Vegetables

Carrot Tzimmes

❖　❖　❖

THIS IS A VERY TRADITIONAL DISH THAT IS SERVED IN MANY
A JEWISH HOME, ESPECIALLY ON ROSH HASHANAH,
BECAUSE IT IS SWEET.

In a large pot, place the apple juice, orange juice, and lemon juice. Add the salt, sugar, cardamom, and peppercorns. Add the water. Bring to a boil and add the meat. Cook until almost tender. Add the carrots and potatoes. Cook until tender, and almost all the liquid has been absorbed.

For a stronger flavor, adjust with salt and lemon juice–just a little at a time.

Serve hot.

YIELD: 10 SERVINGS

12 ounces frozen apple juice, undiluted

4   ounces frozen orange juice, undiluted

1/4 cup fresh lemon juice

2   teaspoons salt

1/2 cup brown sugar, or 2 teaspoons Sweet 'n Low

1/4 teaspoon cardamom

8   whole black peppercorns

1/2 cup water

2   pounds sirloin or filet mignon, cut into small chunks (optional)

1   pound sliced carrots, fresh or frozen

4   large sweet potatoes, cut into chunks

Carrot Pudding

❖   ❖   ❖

THIS IS AN OLD FAMILY FAVORITE, SERVED AT ALMOST EVERY
HOLIDAY MEAL, OR ANY OTHER TIME DURING THE YEAR.
THE CHILDREN LOVE IT.

1½ cups flour

1½ teaspoons baking soda

1 teaspoon baking powder

½ teaspoon salt

½ teaspoon cinnamon

½ teaspoon nutmeg

⅛ teaspoon cloves

¼ pound butter or margarine

½ cup oil

½ cup brown sugar

2 egg yolks

1¾ cups grated carrots

¼ cup fresh lemon juice

grated rind of 1 lemon

3 egg whites

Sift the flour, baking soda, baking powder, salt, and spices together. Combine the butter, oil, brown sugar, and egg yolks in a food processor. Blend well. Add the carrots, lemon juice, and rind and blend once again. Incorporate the flour mixture. Remove batter to a large bowl. Beat the egg whites until stiff and fold into the batter.

Pour into a 4½-cup greased ring mold or an 8½ × 11-inch baking pan. Place in refrigerator overnight. Remove from refrigerator and allow to stand at room temperature for ½ hour prior to baking.

Bake at 350°F for 45 to 60 minutes. Test with a toothpick at 45 minutes.

This may be frozen unbaked. When ready to bake, remove from freezer and allow to stand at room temperature for about 1 hour before baking. It may be necessary to allow additional time for baking if not thawed completely.

YIELD: 6 TO 8 SERVINGS

Sweet-and-Sour Cabbage

❖ ❖ ❖

IT TOOK ME SOME TIME TO PERFECT THIS RECIPE. I HAVE
PREPARED THIS FOR MY DIABETIC HUSBAND AND FRIENDS,
AND THEY WERE JUST DELIGHTED. I NO LONGER USE THE
SUGAR CALLED FOR—ONLY THE SWEET 'N LOW.

Place all the ingredients, except the meat and the cabbage, in a very large pot. Bring to a boil and add the meat. Cook slowly. When meat is almost tender, add all of the cabbage. If more liquid is needed, add a little water.

After the cabbage has cooked for a short time, adjust the seasonings—lemon juice and salt for the sweet-and-sour flavor. Salt is the trick in achieving the sweet-and-sour flavor, but be careful—just a little at a time.

Simmer for an additional 45 minutes.

Remove the bay leaf after removing from the heat.

YIELD: 3 QUARTS

2	large cans (28 ounces each) plum tomatoes, including the juice
1	tomato can filled with water
1/2	cup fresh lemon juice
1	12-ounce can frozen apple juice, undiluted
5	teaspoons salt
1	cup raisins (light or dark)
6	whole peppercorns
1	bay leaf
1/4	teaspoon ground cardamom
1/4	teaspoon ground coriander
1/2	cup brown sugar, or 2 teaspoons Sweet 'n Low*
1	large round-bone chuck pot roast, or 2 to 3 pounds of boneless chuck for stewing
2	large heads of cabbage, coarsely sliced

*If you are omitting sugar and using a sweetener, you must not use an aspartame product when cooking.

Potato Kugel or Kugelettes

❖ ❖ ❖

A VARIATION ON A TIME-TESTED THEME. THE LITTLE POTATO
KUGELETTES MAKE A GREAT PRESENTATION WHEN PLACED
AROUND POULTRY OR BEEF.

6   *large white potatoes*

1   *onion*

2   *eggs, or ¹/₂ cup egg substitute*

2   *egg whites*

2   *tablespoons peanut oil*

¹/₄   *cup matzo meal*

¹/₂   *teaspoon baking powder*

¹/₂   *teaspoon garlic powder*

1   *teaspoon salt*

¹/₈   *teaspoon white pepper*

    peanut oil for muffin tins or baking dish

Preheat oven to 350°F.

Peel potatoes and onion. Cut up and place in a food processor. (If not using immediately, place in cold water.)

Process with steel blade with on-off pulsing motion. Do not allow mixture to become too thin. Put in a large strainer and press out liquid. Then pour some cold water over the potatoes and press out liquid once more.

Transfer to a large mixing bowl. Beat eggs and egg whites until thick. Add to potato and onion mixture. Add the 2 tablespoons of peanut oil and then add the matzo meal, baking powder, and seasonings. Blend well.

Grease medium-size muffin tins or a 9 × 13-inch baking dish very generously with peanut oil. Heat for a few minutes in the preheated oven. Pour potato mixture over the hot oil. Return to oven and bake for 1 hour, until crispy and brown.

YIELD: 12 SERVINGS OF KUGEL, OR 16 TO 18 KUGELETTES

Potato Latkes

❖ ❖ ❖

THE FOOD PROCESSOR HAS ELIMINATED THE GRATING OF THE
POTATOES AND HAS MADE THIS TRADITIONAL HOLIDAY
FAVORITE SO SIMPLE. HAPPY HANUKKAH!

Peel potatoes and onion. Cut up and place in a food processor.
(If not using immediately, place in cold water).

Process with steel blade with on-off pulsing motion. Do not
allow mixture to become too thin. Put in a large strainer and
press out liquid. Then pour some cold water over the potatoes
and press out liquid once more. Transfer to a large mixing bowl.
Beat eggs and egg whites until thick. Add to potato mixture. Add
flour, baking powder, and seasonings. Blend well.

Heat oil in a frying pan. When ready, drop batter from a large
metal cooking spoon. This will give you an oval shape. Fry over
moderate to high heat until brown, turning to brown other side.
Remove from frying pan and drain excess oil on paper towels.

Serve with sour cream or applesauce.

These may be made in advance and frozen. To freeze, place
singly on a baking sheet, freeze, and then place in a plastic bag.
To reheat, defrost. Place on baking sheet or stand pancakes up
in a loaf pan and bake in preheated 450°F oven until crisp.

YIELD: 18 LATKES

6   large white potatoes

1   large onion

2   eggs, or $^1/_2$ cup egg
    substitute

2   egg whites

$^1/_3$ cup flour or matzo
    meal

1   teaspoon baking pow-
    der

$^1/_2$ teaspoon garlic pow-
    der

1   teaspoon salt

$^1/_2$ teaspoon white pep-
    per

    peanut oil for frying

Oven-Roasted Potatoes

❖ ❖ ❖

WHEN I MAKE THESE, I NEVER TRY TO JUDGE WHAT I NEED
PER PERSON. I MAKE TREMENDOUS QUANTITIES AND THEY
JUST SEEM TO DISAPPEAR. THESE ARE DELICIOUS AND
PRETTY LOW IN FAT, IF YOU ARE NOT TOO
GENEROUS WITH THE OLIVE OIL.

6 to 8 medium-size bak-
ing potatoes,
scrubbed and cut into
wedges*

Soak the potato wedges in cold water for about ¹/₂ hour. Drain potatoes in a colander and pat dry with paper toweling.

1   package Lipton's
Savory Herb & Garlic
Mix

Preheat oven to 375°F. Spray a large deep pan with olive oil or a vegetable cooking spray.

olive oil

paprika

Place the potato wedges in the pan and sprinkle with the Lipton's mix.

Toss well to cover the potatoes and sprinkle with olive oil. Shake paprika over the entire pan. This not only adds flavor but aids in the browning.

Roast potatoes, uncovered, for about 1 hour, tossing frequently so that they are well browned on all sides. If you find that you need a little more oil, use it sparingly. You do not want a soggy wedge.

YIELD: 6 SERVINGS

*I also use small red potatoes (when available), cutting them into halves or quarters.

Candied Sweet Potatoes

❖　❖　❖

THIS IS A RECIPE HANDED DOWN FROM MY MOTHER,
GRANDMA IDA, AND WAS ALWAYS A HIT WITH THE FAMILY.

In a covered pan, steam the potatoes in a small amount of water, just until you can easily remove the skin.

Cut the potatoes in halves or quarters and place them in a well-greased baking dish. Set aside.

To make the glaze, combine the brown sugar, orange juice, and butter in a medium-size saucepan and cook for at least 5 minutes, or until clear.

Pour this glaze over the potatoes and bake in a 350°F oven for 45 minutes, basting several times. When done, they should be well glazed or candied.

Note: For a sugar-free recipe, omit the glaze and use a sugar-free maple pancake syrup (available in any supermarket). Sprinkle potatoes with a little orange juice and pour the syrup over the potatoes. Bake as you would the others.

YIELD: 10 TO 12 SERVINGS

8　*medium-size sweet potatoes*

GLAZE:

1　*cup solidly packed brown sugar*

¹/₃　cup fresh orange juice

1　*tablespoon butter*

Oven-Roasted Asparagus

❖ ❖ ❖

I PREFER THIS METHOD TO STOVE-TOP OR
MICROWAVE COOKING.

1   *pound fresh, peeled asparagus (very thin)*

1   *tablespoon garlic oil*

     fresh lemon juice (optional)

Use the smallest oven-to-table dish that will hold the asparagus comfortably. Pour the oil into the pan and then place the asparagus.

Preheat oven to 400°F. Roast asparagus in center of oven for about 6 minutes. Turn and roast an additional 5 minutes.

Remove from oven. Sprinkle with fresh lemon juice and serve immediately.

YIELD: 4 SERVINGS

Baked Tomatoes

❖ ❖ ❖

A BEAUTIFUL GARNISH FOR ANY ENTRÉE.
ONE OF MY FAVORITES.

Place the tomato halves on a greased cookie sheet. Sprinkle with seasoned crumbs, Parmesan cheese, oregano, and a little more crumbs. Dot with butter.

Bake at 325°F for about 30 minutes.

YIELD: **12 SERVINGS**

6 *medium-size toma- toes, cut in half*

seasoned bread crumbs

Parmesan cheese

oregano

dots of butter

Eggplant Relish

❖ ❖ ❖

SLIGHTLY PUNGENT—AND WONDERFUL! I SERVE THIS AS AN
APPETIZER OR AS A SIDE DISH.

1	medium-size eggplant
1	medium-size onion, coarsely chopped
2	teaspoons curry powder
1/4	teaspoon ground ginger
6	tablespoons peanut oil
1/2	teaspoon salt
2	teaspoons fresh lemon juice
2	tablespoons mango chutney

Cut the eggplant in half. Cut each half lengthwise into 4 slices. Cut each slice into 1-inch-wide pieces and put in a bowl. Add the onion, curry powder, and ginger. Toss to mix.

In a large skillet, heat the oil over high heat. Add the eggplant mixture and sauté for about 3 minutes, tossing frequently. Reduce heat to moderate and cook, tossing frequently, until the eggplant is tender and browned—about 25 minutes. Remove from the heat and stir in the salt, lemon juice, and chutney.

Serve hot, chilled, or at room temperature as a side dish.

This can also be served as an appetizer with pita bread triangles.

YIELD: 6 SERVINGS

Cold Marinated Vegetables

❖ ❖ ❖

THESE ARE A MARVELOUS COMPLEMENT TO ANY MEAL AND MAKE A BEAUTIFUL PRESENTATION. LEFTOVERS HOLD UP QUITE WELL IN THE REFRIGERATOR.

The amounts of vegetables will vary according to your needs. I usually use a selection of three different veggies–small carrots, petite green beans, whole baby beets, artichoke hearts, cauliflower or broccoli florets, large white mushroom caps, or petite green peas.

The only vegetables needing to be blanched (just slightly cooked) will be the carrots and green beans. You can use the frozen or fresh.

Each selection of vegetables should be marinated separately for at least 2 days. Just before arranging them on your serving dish, drain them for at least 10 minutes.

For the marinade, I would suggest my Marinade for Raw Vegetables or any light vinaigrette of your choice. Pour just enough of the marinade over the vegetables to flavor them. Too much will make them very oily. Place in the refrigerator.

I use containers with tight lids and invert them from time to time, never opening them until ready to serve. (Drain well before serving.)

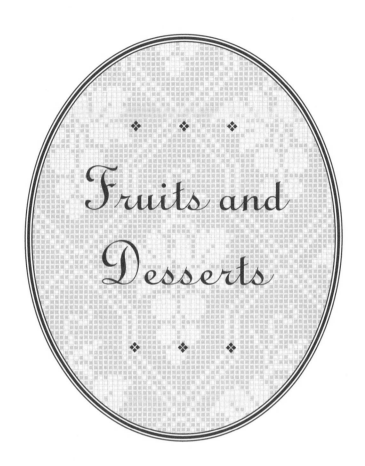

Fruits and
Desserts

Grandma Doralee's Applesauce

❖　❖　❖

WE LOVE THIS CHUNKY APPLESAUCE. WE USE IT FOR A SIDE DISH AT DINNER, OR AS A DESSERT.

Place all the ingredients in a large casserole. Cover tightly and place in a 350°F oven for 1 hour.

Remove from oven and allow to cool. When cool, remove stick cinnamon and set aside.

This may be served as is, chunky, or processed in a food processor with short pulsing motions; just enough to give you a thick sauce. Return the stick cinnamon to the sauce and refrigerate.

This freezes very well.

YIELD: **8 TO 10 SERVINGS**

12 McIntosh apples, cored, peeled, and cut into chunks

3 to 4 pieces of stick cinnamon

1/8 teaspoon ground cloves

1/4 cup water

Baked Apples

❖　❖　❖

I ALWAYS TRY TO HAVE THESE IN THE REFRIGERATOR DURING
APPLE SEASON. ANOTHER WONDERFUL DESSERT THAT
WON'T RUIN YOUR DIET.

6	large apples (I always use McIntosh)
1/2	cup raisins
	ground cinnamon, cloves, and nutmeg
1	can diet cola

Preheat oven to 375°F.

Core apples to 1/2 inch from the bottom. Pare about 1/3 inch from the top.

Arrange apples in baking dish. Fill centers with a few raisins. Sprinkle with the cinnamon, cloves, and nutmeg. Pour the cola over the apples and add the balance of the raisins to the baking dish.

Bake for about 1 hour, or until tender. Do not overbake, as they will burst. Remove from oven and baste with liquid in pan.

Serve hot or cold, always basting first with a little liquid.

YIELD: 6 SERVINGS

Banana Dessert (Fat-Free and Sugar-Free)

❖ ❖ ❖

THIS IS A MARVELOUS LOW-FAT, SUGAR-FREE DESSERT. YOU
CAN ADD ALMOST ANY FRUIT, BUT REMEMBER, IT MUST BE
FROZEN FIRST. AS FRUITS START TO RIPEN, CUT THEM UP,
PLACE IN A PLASTIC BAG, AND FREEZE. THIS CAME FROM
THE KITCHEN OF SYLVIA SILVERMAN.

Place all the ingredients in a food processor and process until
very thick. Spoon into dessert dishes and serve at once.

Leftovers can be frozen, but are a little slushy when defrosted.

YIELD: 3 TO 4 SERVINGS

2   frozen bananas, cut
    into pieces.

¹⁄₃ cup orange juice

¹⁄₂ teaspoon vanilla
    extract

1   packet sugar substi-
    tute

    dash of cinnamon
    and dash of nutmeg

Chocolate Mousse

❖ ❖ ❖

THIS WILL DELIGHT ALL CHOCOLATE LOVERS. REMEMBER,
WHEN WHIPPING CREAM, ALWAYS HAVE THE BOWL AND THE
BEATERS ICE COLD. DO NOT USE A FOOD PROCESSOR;
USE YOUR ELECTRIC MIXER.

1 pint whipping cream	Beat cream until stiff. Add melted chocolate, egg yolks, orange rind, and liqueur and blend well.
12 ounces semisweet chocolate, melted	
2 eggs, separated (room temperature)	Beat egg whites with sugar into a stiff meringue. Fold into cream mixture.
1 teaspoon grated orange rind	
1/3 cup orange-chocolate liqueur or any liqueur of your choice that blends well with chocolate	Pour into a pretty crystal bowl. Cover with plastic wrap and place in freezer. Remove at least 30 minutes before serving.

YIELD: 8 TO 10 SERVINGS |
| 1/2 cup sugar | |

Coffee Ice Cream

❖ ❖ ❖

MY ABSOLUTE FAVORITE ICE CREAM IS COFFEE. REMEMBER,
WHEN WHIPPING CREAM, ALWAYS HAVE THE BOWL AND THE
BEATERS ICE COLD. DO NOT USE A FOOD PROCESSOR;
USE YOUR ELECTRIC MIXER.

Beat cream until stiff. Add instant coffee, egg yolks, and vanilla, and continue beating until well blended. Beat egg whites with sugar into a stiff meringue. Fold into cream mixture.

Pour into a pretty crystal bowl. Cover with plastic wrap and place in freezer. Remove at least 30 minutes before serving.

YIELD: 8 TO 10 SERVINGS

2   pints whipping cream

4   eggs, separated (room temperature)

4   tablespoons instant coffee

1   teaspoon vanilla extract

1   scant cup sugar

Cranberry-Orange Relish

❖ ❖ ❖

THIS CAN BE SERVED HOT OR COLD. I BELIEVE THIS CAME
FROM THE KITCHEN OF MY DEAR FRIEND, VIVIAN GILL.

1   *1-pound package
fresh cranberries*

1   *cup sugar, or
5 teaspoons
Sweet 'n Low**

3   *very large sweet
apples, coarsely
chopped*

15 *ounces orange mar-
malade (or sugar-free
marmalade)*

4   *navel oranges, rind
and all, finely
chopped*

1   *1-pound package
fresh cranberries, fine-
ly chopped*

Preheat the oven to 350°F.

Place the cranberries, sugar, and apples in a 4- to 6-quart casserole. Cover tightly with aluminum foil. Bake for 45 minutes.
Remove from oven; do not remove the foil. Allow to cool.

When cool add the remaining ingredients and blend well.

This also freezes well.

*Do not use an aspartame product when cooking or baking.

Lemon Ice Cream Pie

❖ ❖ ❖

I LOVE THE GREAT LEMONY FLAVOR AND IT CAN BE MADE
AHEAD OF TIME AND FROZEN.

Preheat oven to 325°F.

Melt the butter in a 10-inch pie plate and pour the flour and
powdered sugar over the melted butter. Mix well and press into
place. Prick with a fork.

Bake for 15 to 20 minutes. Remove from oven and let cool.

Beat cream until peaky. Add sugar, yolks, and juice. Beat until
thick. Set aside.

Beat egg whites into a stiff meringue. Fold into cream mixture,
adding the rind at the same time.

Pour into cooled crust. Sprinkle with toasted chopped pecans or
toasted sliced almonds.

Place in the freezer. After it is frozen, cover with plastic wrap.
Remove from freezer 30 minutes before serving.

CRUST:

$^1/_4$ pound butter

1   cup flour

$^1/_4$ cup powdered sugar

FILLING:

1   pint whipping cream

$^1/_3$ cup sugar

2   eggs, separated (room
    temperature)

2   lemons, juice and
    grated rind ($^1/_2$
    cup juice)

Strawberries à la Marny

❖ ❖ ❖

THIS RECIPE CAME FROM A VERY FINE RESTAURANT IN THE
SAN DIEGO AREA AND WAS A SMASHING SUCCESS
WHENEVER SERVED.

16 extra-large straw-
    berries

SAUCE:

4 tablespoons dairy
   sour cream (fat-free
   or light)

4 tablespoons dairy
   whip (regular or
   light)

2 tablespoons brown
   sugar

1 tablespoon Grand
   Marnier

2 tablespoons Curaçao

1/2 tablespoon dark rum

Combine the sour cream with dairy whip; blend brown sugar into it. Add Grand Marnier; whip. Add Curaçao; whip, and finish up with rum.

Fashion a mound of crushed ice in a crystal bowl. Place the berries on the crushed ice.

Serve the sauce in individual sherbet or wide champagne glasses and dip the berries into it.

Other fruits in season can also be used with the same sauce, although the berries are the most attractive.

YIELD: SERVES 4

Baked Peaches with Raspberry Sauce

❖ ❖ ❖

THIS CAN BE SERVED AS A DESSERT OR AS A SIDE DISH WITH
A MEAL. I LOVE TO SERVE HOT FRUIT OF ANY KIND.
TRY PEARS NEXT TIME.

Place each peach half, cut side up, in a baking dish and sprinkle with cinnamon, brown sugar, a touch of ground cloves and nutmeg, and a little rum flavoring (optional). Dot with butter.

Place in a 375°F oven until thoroughly heated (about 20 minutes).

Fresh peaches in season, or canned if out of season

cinnamon

brown sugar

ground cloves

nutmeg

rum flavoring (optional)

If using fresh peaches, they should be peeled, halved, and pitted.

Serve as is or with the following sauce:

Combine raspberries and lemon juice in a processor and process until smooth. Strain and discard seeds. Cover and refrigerate.

1 package frozen raspberries in light syrup, slightly thawed

3 teaspoons fresh lemon juice

Hot Fruit Compote

❖ ❖ ❖

THIS DELICIOUS FRUIT COMPOTE ACCOMPANIES EVERY
HOLIDAY MEAL. IT CAN BE SERVED HOT OR AT
ROOM TEMPERATURE.

1	24-ounce can peaches
1	24-ounce can apricot halves
1	16-ounce can pineapple chunks
1	16-ounce can cherry pie filling
¹/₄	cup brown sugar
¹/₄	cup liqueur (orange, cherry, or apricot)
¹/₂	cup toasted sliced almonds

Preheat oven to 350°F.

Drain peaches, apricots, and pineapple and combine with pie filling, sugar, and liqueur.

Pour ingredients into an ovenproof casserole, cover with toasted almonds, and bake for 1 hour.

YIELD: 10 SERVINGS

Italian Plum Compote

❖ ❖ ❖

DELICIOUS AS A COMPLEMENT TO ANY MEAL. THIS RECIPE
WAS GIVEN TO ME MANY YEARS AGO BY MY BELOVED
FRIEND, BESS BROWN.

Cook the plums, oranges, raisins, and the sugar for about 1 hour over low heat.

Remove from heat and add lemon juice and nuts.

YIELD: 10 TO 12 SERVINGS

4 *pounds Italian plums, pitted and chopped very coarsely*

2 *navel oranges, chopped (rind and all)*

1 *cup raisins*

2 *cups sugar*

   juice of 1 lemon

³/₄ *cup chopped pecans or walnuts*

Lemon Bread Pudding

❖ ❖ ❖

BECAUSE THIS WAS ONE OF MY MOTHER'S OLD RECIPES, I
WANTED TO INCLUDE IT. I REMEMBER ENJOYING
THIS AS A CHILD.

PUDDING:

5   slices stale white
bread, cut into large
pieces

1   cup sugar

4   eggs, separated

1   lemon, juice and grated rind

2   cups milk

3   tablespoons butter,
melted

MERINGUE:

4   egg whites

1   cup sugar

   juice of 1 lemon

Place the pieces of bread in a greased oblong Pyrex baking dish.

Combine the sugar, egg yolks, juice and rind, milk, and melted butter and pour over the bread.

Bake in a 350°F oven for 30 minutes. Test to see if done.

Meanwhile, beat the egg whites for the meringue until foamy. Gradually add sugar and beat into stiff peaks. Fold in lemon juice. Remove pudding from oven and spread the meringue carefully over the hot pudding.

Return pudding to oven to brown. Watch carefully.

YIELD: 9 SERVINGS

Tapioca Dessert

❖   ❖   ❖

MY MOTHER ALWAYS TOPPED THIS WITH CRUSHED
PINEAPPLE, AND IT'S ALWAYS BEEN ONE OF MY FAVORITE
DESSERTS. THIS IS HER ORIGINAL RECIPE.

Beat egg whites into a stiff meringue and set aside.

Put remaining ingredients, except vanilla, in a large saucepan
and bring to a boil, stirring constantly until it thickens.

When thick, remove from heat. Cool slightly and add beaten egg
whites and vanilla.

Spoon into dessert dishes and serve with any fruit sauce.

YIELD: 4 TO 6 SERVINGS

2   eggs, separated (room
     temperature)

1   extra egg white

¹/₄ cup tapioca

2   cups milk

¹/₄ teaspoon salt

¹/₃ cup sugar

1   teaspoon vanilla
     extract

Cookies,
Cakes, and
Pastry

COOKIE NOTES

From the standpoint of flavor, it is best to use butter when making cookies; however, half butter and half margarine may be used.

Under no circumstances should you use light butters or margarines. They contain too much liquid and will not yield good results.

For the most satisfactory cookies, always beat butter, sugar, and eggs until very light and creamy; then add the other ingredients and beat only until well blended.

I always use baking parchment on my cookie sheets, instead of greasing the sheets. This prevents the cookies from browning too fast.

After cookies are cool, store them in a tight container. Save your coffee cans for storage of cookies.

Most cookies can be frozen. However, for maximum flavor, I would suggest freezing no longer than three months.

When freezing cookies, along with waxed paper between the layers, I suggest a sheet of paper toweling to absorb moisture; also, a doubled sheet of paper toweling on top of full container, placed right under the cover.

Most cookies will travel well. If they are tightly packed, they should arrive at their destination safely.

For the most satisfactory results, please follow the recipes carefully.

Grandma Doralee's Butter Crisps

❖ ❖ ❖

THIS HAS BECOME MY SIGNATURE COOKIE. IT IS EVERYONE'S
FAVORITE, ESPECIALLY MY GRANDCHILDREN. IF GRANDMA IS
COMING, SO ARE THE BUTTER CRISPS.

2¼ cups flour

1   cup sifted powdered
    sugar

½   teaspoon salt

½   pound butter, or half
    butter–half
    margarine

1   egg, beaten until light

2   teaspoons vanilla
    extract

1   egg white, slightly
    beaten with 1 table-
    spoon water

    cinnamon and sugar

Place flour, sugar, salt and butter in a food processor with the
steel blade. Blend until mealy.

Sprinkle 2 tablespoons of the beaten egg and the vanilla over the
mixture in the processor and process until mixture forms a ball.
Remove dough from processor and shape into 5 long rolls,
about 1¼ inches in diameter. Wrap in waxed paper, place on a
cookie sheet, and place in freezer. When frozen, place rolls in a
plastic bag and store in freezer until you are ready to bake them.
Should you want to bake them instead of storing them for later,
they should be frozen slightly in order to slice easily.

When ready to bake, preheat oven to 400°F. Slice the cookies
about ¼ inch thick, brush with beaten egg white, sprinkle with
cinnamon and sugar, and place on cookie sheet covered with
baking parchment. These cookies burn very rapidly, that is why
I suggest using parchment paper.

Bake for 5 to 10 minutes. Allow to cool on parchment and store
in an airtight container.

YIELD: 85 COOKIES

Chocolate Chip Cookies

❖　❖　❖

OH, HOW MY KIDS USED TO LOVE TO MAKE THESE
BY THEMSELVES!

Preheat oven to 375°F.

Combine butter, sugars, and eggs and beat well. Sift dry ingredients together and add to the butter mixture. Mix well. Add the vanilla, hot water, chocolate chips, and nuts. Mix well once again.

Drop by teaspoon or small scoop onto parchment-covered cookie sheet.

Bake for 10 to 12 minutes.

Allow to cool before removing from pan.

YIELD: 60 TO 72 COOKIES (DEPENDING UPON SIZE)

$^1/_2$　pound butter, margarine, or vegetable shortening

$^3/_4$　cup white sugar

$^3/_4$　cup brown sugar

2　whole eggs, beaten

2$^1/_4$ cups flour

1　teaspoon baking soda

1　teaspoon salt

1　teaspoon vanilla extract

1　tablespoon hot water

1　large package semi-sweet chocolate chips

1　cup chopped nuts (optional)

Chocolate Butter Cookies (White Persian Caps)

❖ ❖ ❖

THESE MAKE A STUNNING ADDITION TO A SWEET TABLE.

12	tablespoons butter
¹/₂	cup sugar
1	egg yolk
1	teaspoon vanilla or almond extract
¹/₂	cup coarsely chopped nuts (optional)
8	ounces semisweet chocolate chips (optional)
1¹/₂	cups flour
¹/₃	cup Droste's cocoa
	Hershey's Kisses (the white spiral, not the dark chocolate)

Preheat oven to 375°F.

Combine all the ingredients except flour, cocoa, and Kisses and blend well. Add the flour and cocoa and blend once again.

Form 1-inch balls and place on a cookie sheet lined with baking parchment. Bake for 6 to 7 minutes, or until set. Do not overbake.

Remove from oven. Immediately place a white spiral Hershey Kiss in the center of each cookie, depressing lightly so that it holds. Cool until chocolate kiss is once again firm.

VARIATION:

Make the cookies using the nuts and chocolate chips. When slightly cool, dust lightly with powdered sugar. Omit the Kisses.

YIELD: APPROXIMATELY 60 COOKIES

Button Drops

❖   ❖   ❖

THESE WILL JUST MELT IN YOUR MOUTH—SO DELICIOUS!

Cream the butter, sugar, vanilla, and salt until light and fluffy.
Add yolks and mix well. Add flour and nuts and blend well.

Form into 1-inch balls. Place 1^1/$_2$ inches apart on a parchment-
covered cookie sheet. Press down in center. Brush with slightly
beaten egg white.

Preheat oven to 350°F and bake for about 15 minutes, or until
lightly browned.

YIELD: ABOUT 75 COOKIES

^{1}/$_2$ *pound butter*

^{3}/$_4$ *cup sugar*

1   *teaspoon vanilla*
      extract

^{1}/$_2$ *teaspoon salt*

2   *large eggs, separated*

1^1/$_3$ *cups flour*

1^1/$_2$ *cups chopped nuts*

Cinnamon Roll-Ups

❖ ❖ ❖

THERE IS ABSOLUTELY NOTHING BETTER WITH A CUP OF TEA
OR COFFEE! ONE OF MY FAVORITES.

2½ cups flour

½ pound butter

12 ounces cream cheese

cinnamon and sugar

1 egg beaten with 3
tablespoons water
(egg wash)

1 to 2 cups ground
pecans

Preheat oven to 350°F.

Place the flour, butter, and cheese in a food processor and blend very well. Form dough into a ball. Wrap in waxed paper and place in refrigerator overnight.

Roll dough into circles—the size depending upon the size of the roll-up desired. The larger the circle, the larger the roll-up will be. Sprinkle with cinnamon and sugar and ground nuts. Cut circle into wedges resembling a pinwheel. Roll up each wedge from the outside into the center.

Brush with the egg wash and sprinkle with cinnamon and sugar.

Place rolls on a cookie sheet lined with baking parchment, and bake for 22 to 25 minutes, or until lightly browned.

YIELD: AT LEAST 48 COOKIES

Grandma Doralee's Brownies

❖ ❖ ❖

THIS RECIPE IS MORE THAN FIFTY YEARS OLD, AND STILL IS IN GREAT DEMAND WHEREVER I GO. I AIM TO PLEASE!

Preheat oven to 350°F.

Melt the butter and chocolate in a large bowl. Add the eggs, sugar, vanilla, flour, and nuts. Blend well.

Pour into a well-greased and lightly floured pan, approximately 11 × 13 inches. Bake for 20 minutes.

Remove from oven. Cool and cut into desired size.

Note: If traveling with these, I suggest you use the E.Z. Foil Ready-Mix Cake Pans (12¼ × 8¼ × 1¼ inches), and do not cut them until ready to serve.

YIELD: 24 TO 36 PIECES, DEPENDING UPON SIZE OF BROWNIES

1/2 pound butter

4 squares unsweetened baking chocolate

4 whole eggs

2 cups sugar

2 teaspoons vanilla extract

1 cup flour

1 cup chopped nuts (optional)

Brownie Cupcakes

❖ ❖ ❖

MUCH LIKE A BROWNIE, BUT JUST DIFFERENT ENOUGH TO
MAKE A HIT WITH THE YOUNGER SET. GIDEON LOVED THESE.

2	squares unsweetened baking chocolate
1/4	pound butter
2	eggs
1	cup sugar
1	teaspoon vanilla extract
1/3	cup milk
2/3	cup flour
	chocolate sprinkles (Jimmies)

Preheat oven to 350°F.

Melt chocolate and butter together in a large Pyrex bowl. When melted, add the eggs, sugar, and vanilla and blend well. Add the milk, and then the flour. Blend well.

Fill miniature muffin tins with paper cups. Pour the chocolate mixture into the paper cups and cover with chocolate sprinkles.

Bake for 15 minutes.

YIELD: **24 MINIATURE CUPCAKES**

Cream Cheese Brownies

❖ ❖ ❖

VERY RICH, BUT THEY JUST MELT IN YOUR MOUTH.
LAURIE LOVES THESE.

Preheat oven to 350°F.

Melt the butter and chocolate. Add eggs, sugar, and vanilla. Blend well. Add flour and baking powder. Blend well once again. Pour into a greased 9-inch square pan. Set aside.

Blend the cream cheese, sugar, vanilla, and egg and pour over the brownie mixture. Bake for 35 to 40 minutes.

Note: If you would like a little color in the cheese mixture, use a tiny bit of green coloring and substitute peppermint extract for the vanilla.

YIELD: 36 1 1/2-INCH SQUARES

1/4 pound butter

2 squares unsweetened baking chocolate

2 eggs

1 cup sugar

1 teaspoon vanilla extract

1/2 cup flour

1/4 teaspoon baking powder

8 ounces cream cheese

1/2 cup sugar

1/2 teaspoon vanilla extract

1 egg

Florentines

❖ ❖ ❖

THESE DON'T LAST VERY LONG. THEY JUST DISAPPEAR.

1   cup sugar

2¹/₂ cups sliced almonds

¹/₄ pound butter, melted

5   tablespoons flour

2   egg whites, slightly
    beaten

    dash of salt

¹/₂ teaspoon vanilla
    extract

Preheat oven to 350°F.

Toss sugar and almonds together. Stir in melted butter. Stir in flour, egg whites, salt, and vanilla until well blended.

Line cookie sheets with baking parchment. Drop by spoonfuls onto sheets about 2 inches apart.

Bake one sheet at a time for 10 minutes, or until golden brown around the edges and bottom.

Cool on the parchment.

Option: When cool, brush one end with melted semisweet chocolate. Place on waxed paper and allow to harden.

YIELD: WILL DEPEND UPON SIZE OF COOKIE

Doralee's Preserve Squares

❖ ❖ ❖

WONDERFULLY RICH!

In food processor, combine everything but preserves. Process into a smooth ball.

Press half of the dough into a greased jelly roll type pan, approximately $11^{1}/_{2} \times 16 \times 1$ inches.

First spread one preserve, and then spread the other preserve on top of it. Cover with remaining dough. Press with hands until it meets the edges of the pan.

Sprinkle with cinnamon and sugar.

Bake at 350° for 45 minutes or until lightly brown.

Cool before cutting into desired size square.

YIELD: **42 TO 48 SQUARES**

1 *pound butter*

4 *egg yolks*

2 *cups sugar*

4 *cups flour*

2 *cups ground pecans*

10 *ounces apricot preserves*

10 *ounces raspberry preserves*

cinnamon and sugar

Grandma Doralee's Strudel

❖ ❖ ❖

THIS IS ALWAYS A "MUST" ON EVERY DESSERT BUFFET.

12 ounces cream cheese

½ pound butter (or half butter, half margarine)

2 cups flour

FILLING:

2 Granny Smith apples, cut up into chunks

1' cup chopped pecans

1 cup raisins

12 ounces orange marmalade

1 cup shredded coconut (optional)

Place the cold cream cheese and butter in a food processor. Add the flour and blend well into a smooth ball. Place in refrigerator or freeze until ready to use.

Preheat oven to 400°F.

Combine the filling ingredients in the food processor and process until well chopped. Mixture will be thick.

Divide dough into several parts; roll each part (one at a time) into a narrow rectangle (about 4 inches wide) and spread with the filling.

Roll each rectangle carefully, folding in the sides from the very beginning.

Place rolls on cookie sheets covered with baking parchment.

Bake for about 45 minutes, or until light brown.

Cool before slicing. When possible, use a serrated knife. For smaller pieces, cut straight across. For larger pieces, cut on the diagonal.

Before serving, sprinkle with powdered sugar. Place in paper cups.

Note: For a low-fat, no-sugar variation, use low-fat cottage cheese, corn oil margarine, and sugar-free preserves.

Jelly Kichel

❖ ❖ ❖

**ANOTHER FAMILY FAVORITE! FROM THE KITCHEN OF IDA
(AUNTIE IDA) DRAY.**

¹/₄	*pound butter*
¹/₄	*pound margarine*
1¹/₄	*cups sugar*
6	*eggs*
2	*teaspoons vanilla extract*
1	*teaspoon lemon extract, or ¹/₂ teaspoon butter-flavor extract*
¹/₂	*teaspoon almond extract*
4¹/₂	*cups flour*
¹/₂	*teaspoon salt*
2¹/₂	*teaspoons baking powder*
	apricot preserves
	raspberry preserves
	ground nuts
	cinnamon and sugar

Cream the butter, margarine, and sugar well. Add the eggs and extracts and cream very well. Combine flour, salt, and baking powder and add to the creamed mixture. Do not overbeat. Mixture should not be too thick or too loose.

Place in a large bowl, cover with plastic wrap, and refrigerate overnight.

When ready to bake, place the whole mound of batter on a board and knead back and forth several times. Cut into 6 batches. Take one batch of dough, place on slightly floured board, and roll into a rectangle.

Spread first with apricot preserves; next, the raspberry preserves. Sprinkle entire rectangle with ground nuts and lots of cinnamon and sugar.

Roll up the rectangle in jelly-roll fashion and place on a cookie sheet covered with baking parchment. Tuck the ends under carefully. Repeat this procedure with each section of dough. Place only two rolls on a cookie sheet.

Bake for 30 to 40 minutes, or until brown. If not brown after 40 minutes, raise temperature to 375°F.

Cut while warm.

YIELD: SIX ROLLS YIELD RATHER LARGE SLICES. IF SMALLER SLICES ARE DESIRED, DIVIDE THE BATTER INTO MORE THAN 6 ROLLS.

Hello Dolly Cookies

❖ ❖ ❖

THIS IS A MARVELOUS COOKIE. THE RECIPE WAS ORIGINALLY
GIVEN TO ME BY MY MOTHER, GRANDMA IDA. THIS WAS
THE NAME SHE GAVE IT.

¹/₄ *pound margarine*	
1 *cup graham cracker crumbs*	
1 *cup shredded coconut*	
1 *cup chopped walnuts*	
12 *ounces semisweet chocolate chips*	
1 *14-ounce can condensed milk*	

Preheat oven to 350°F.

Melt margarine in a 9 × 12-inch pan. Pour graham cracker crumbs over melted margarine. Blend well and spread evenly in pan.

Spread coconut over crumbs; then nuts, and then chocolate chips. Pour condensed milk over all, spreading evenly.

Bake for 30 minutes.

Cool before cutting into squares.

YIELD: AT LEAST 48 SQUARES

Aunt Lillian's Kichel

❖ ❖ ❖

THIS KICHEL WILL ALWAYS EVOKE FOND MEMORIES OF AUNT
LILLIAN. SHE ALWAYS SERVED THESE AT HOME, OR BROUGHT
THEM WHEREVER SHE WENT. EVERYONE, BUT EVERYONE,
LOVED AUNT LILLIAN'S KICHEL. MANDY EVEN GIVES OUT THE
RECIPE AT SOME OF HIS CONCERTS!

Combine butter, sugar, eggs, and sour cream, to which you have added the baking soda. Blend well.

In a separate bowl, combine the above mixture alternately with the flour, to which you have added the cream of tartar and salt. Chill the dough for at least 1 hour.

Preheat oven to 375°F.

Divide the dough into portions easy to handle; on a lightly floured board, roll each portion into a large rectangle, thin enough for you to handle. Cut into vertical strips 2 inches wide, then cut each strip diagonally into pieces approximately 3 inches long.

Place on a cookie sheet lined with baking parchment. Sprinkle with cinnamon and sugar.

Bake for 5 to 8 minutes, until lightly brown around the edges.

YIELD: 60 KICHEL

1/2 pound butter

1 cup sugar

4 eggs

1/4 cup sour cream plus
1 teaspoon baking
soda

4 cups sifted flour plus
1 teaspoon cream of
tartar

dash of salt

cinnamon and sugar

Mandelbrot

❖   ❖   ❖

THIS IS A VERY LIGHT AND CRUNCHY MANDELBROT BROUGHT
TO ME MANY YEARS AGO BY MY DEAR FRIEND, SHIRLEY
EPSTEIN. I HAVE USED ONLY THIS RECIPE SINCE THEN.

½   pound butter

2   tablespoons peanut
    oil

1   cup sugar

3   whole eggs

1   teaspoon vanilla
    extract

1   tablespoon fresh
    lemon juice

    grated rind of 1
    orange

3   cups flour

1   teaspoon baking pow-
    der

¼   teaspoon baking soda

⅛   teaspoon salt

1   cup chopped pecans

    cinnamon and sugar

In a food processor, cream butter, oil, sugar, eggs, vanilla, lemon juice, and orange rind until light and fluffy. Combine flour with baking powder, baking soda, salt, and pecans. Add to butter and egg mixture. Add nuts. Blend well. Refrigerate for several hours.

Preheat oven to 350°F.

Shape into rolls. Size of roll will depend upon the slice you want. Place on cookie sheets covered with baking parchment. Sprinkle with cinnamon and sugar.

Bake for 25 minutes. Remove from oven. Cool slightly and slice. Sprinkle slices with cinnamon and sugar and return to 350° oven for 15 minutes.

Note: This recipe can also be made sugar-free (4 teaspoons Sweet 'n Low). The volume will be less, because of the elimination of sugar.

Cholesterol-free: ¾ cup egg substitute instead of eggs, and corn oil margarine instead of butter.

YIELD: 48 TO 60 PIECES

Kipfel

❖   ❖   ❖

AN OLD VIENNESE MORSEL THAT WILL DELIGHT
YOUR PALATE.

Place the butter, flour, cream cheese, and salt in a food processor and process until it forms a ball.

Wrap in waxed paper and chill in refrigerator for several hours.

Preheat oven to 400°F.

Roll out into a rectangle, fold, and roll again. Cut into 3-inch squares. Fill the centers with thick apricot or raspberry preserves. Bring corners up to center and pinch together.

Place on a cookie sheet lined with baking parchment. Sprinkle lightly with cinnamon and sugar.

Bake for 20 to 30 minutes.

YIELD: 36 PIECES

¹/₂ pound butter

2 cups flour

12 ounces cream cheese

¹/₄ teaspoon salt

apricot or raspberry preserves

cinnamon and sugar

Lemon Torte Squares

❖ ❖ ❖

THESE DISAPPEAR AS FAST AS I PUT THEM ON
THE SWEET TABLE.

CRUST:

¹/₂ pound butter

2 cups flour

¹/₂ cup powdered sugar

TOPPING:

4 eggs, beaten

1³/₄ cups sugar

4 tablespoons flour

1 teaspoon baking powder

¹/₄ teaspoon salt

2 lemons, juice and grated rind

Melt butter in a 9 × 13-inch pan. When melted, sift flour and sugar over the butter. Mix with a fork and press mixture over the bottom of the pan.

Bake at 325°F for 15 to 20 minutes.

While crust bakes, heat the topping ingredients, except the grated rind, until thick. Add rind last and blend well. Pour over the baked crust.

Return to 325°F oven for 30 minutes, until golden brown.

Sprinkle generously with powdered sugar.

This cookie may be frozen, but in single layers. They do not travel well.

YIELD: 36 TO 48 SQUARES

Lemon Mini Tarts

❖ ❖ ❖

OH, SO LEMONY AND LUSCIOUS. ENHANCES
ANY SWEET TABLE.

Preheat oven to 350°F.

Place the butter, cream cheese, and flour in a processor and blend well. Form small balls and press into 1 1/2-inch muffin tins, bringing the dough up the sides. Bake for 30 minutes. Cool on a rack.

Place all the filling ingredients, with the exception of the butter, in a saucepan or double boiler. Blend well with a whisk. Place over low heat and cook, stirring constantly with a wooden spoon, until mixture thickens. As it comes to a boil, remove from heat. Add butter and cool.

Remove tart shells from muffin tins and spoon in the filling.

Refrigerate for several hours or overnight, so that filling becomes firm and flavors blend.

Garnish with toasted chopped almonds or a rosette of whipped cream.

These may be frozen for no longer than 1 month. Freeze and defrost in single layers; however, the empty tart shells can be frozen for 2 to 3 months and filled just before serving.

TART PASTRY:

1/4 pound butter

4 ounces cream cheese

1 cup flour

LEMON FILLING:

2 large eggs

1/2 cup sugar

1/4 cup fresh lemon juice

2 teaspoons grated
fresh lemon rind

4 tablespoons butter
(room temperature)

Mini Fruit Cakes

❖ ❖ ❖

FROM THE KITCHEN OF MY DEAR FRIEND, RUTH WEISS.
I HAVE ALWAYS LOVED THESE—AND THEY'RE SO HEALTHY!

4	extra-large eggs
1	cup raisins
1	cup chopped dates
1	cup chopped walnut
1	cup chopped apricots
1	cup semisweet chocolate chips (optional)

Beat the eggs until light and fluffy. Combine with the remaining ingredients and mix well.

Grease miniature muffin tins. Fill almost to the top.

Preheat oven to 350°F and bake for 20 to 25 minutes.

YIELD: **24** MINI CAKES

Miniature Cheesecakes

❖   ❖   ❖

THESE ARE NOT ONLY DELICIOUS, BUT ADD A LOVELY TOUCH
TO ANY SWEET TABLE.

Preheat oven to 350°F.

Blend all the crust ingredients, then the filling in another bowl.

Place small papers in miniature muffin tins and place about 1 teaspoonful of the crumbs in each cup, pressing down and just slightly up the sides. Fill each cup to the top with the cream cheese filling.

Bake for about 14 minutes. When cool, top with cherry pie filling. Chill until filling is set.

These can be frozen, but do not top with filling until day you are going to serve them.

YIELD: 24 TO 36 PIECES

CRUST:

2   cups graham cracker crumbs

12   tablespoons butter, melted

1/3 cup sugar

FILLING:

2   8-ounce packages cream cheese

2   whole eggs

2/3 cup sugar

2   teaspoons vanilla extract

     grated rind and juice of 1 lemon

TOPPING:

1   21-ounce can cherry pie filling

Doralee's Triple-Threat Delights

❖ ❖ ❖

I DEVELOPED THIS RECIPE SEVERAL YEARS AGO, AFTER
TASTING SOMETHING SIMILAR AT A PRIVATE CLUB. THEY
WOULD NOT DIVULGE THEIR RECIPE, SO I DECIDED TO TRY TO
SEE WHAT I COULD DO. I CAME PRETTY CLOSE. THIS IS
VERY RICH, BUT VERY DELICIOUS!

COOKIE DOUGH:

2¹/₂ cups flour

¹/₂ pound butter or margarine

¹/₂ cup sugar

1 extra-large egg

1 teaspoon vanilla extract

FILLING:

4 eggs

1¹/₂ cups light or dark Karo syrup

1¹/₂ cups sugar

3 tablespoons butter or margarine

1¹/₂ teaspoons vanilla extract

1 cup coarsely chopped pecans

1 cup coarsely chopped blanched almonds

1 cup coarsely chopped walnuts

Preheat oven to 350°F.

Place butter or margarine and flour in a food processor. Blend with the steel blade until crumbly. Add remaining ingredients and process until well blended. Remove from processor and knead into a ball. You can either roll this out to fit a greased 11¹/₂ × 16¹/₂-inch baking pan, or press it into the pan.

Bake for 10 to 15 minutes. Remove from oven.

Combine the filling ingredients and pour over the hot crust. Spread very evenly to distribute the nuts.

Return to 350° oven and bake for 25 minutes, or until filling is firm around the edges and just slightly firm in the center. Cool very well before cutting. Cut into narrow bars.

YIELD: AT LEAST 48 PIECES

Neu Frau Butter Cookies

❖   ❖   ❖

THIS IS AN OLD GERMAN RECIPE THAT WAS GIVEN TO ME
WHEN I WAS A YOUNG GIRL. I LOVED IT, AS DID MY CHILDREN
WHEN THEY WERE YOUNG.

In a food processor, blend butter, sugars, egg yolks, and vanilla until light and creamy. Add flour and salt and blend well.

Divide dough into several long rolls about $1^1/_4$ inches in diameter. Place roll on waxed paper and roll until smooth and round. Wrap each roll in the waxed paper and place in freezer.

When hard, remove and slice about $^1/_4$ inch thick. Place on cookie sheet lined with baking parchment. With your finger, make a depression in each cookie. Brush with slightly beaten egg whites. Place a pecan half on each cookie and depress lightly.

Bake in a 350°F oven for 10 minutes, until lightly brown. Allow to cool on cookie sheet, and then remove very carefully with a metal spatula.

YIELD: 60 TO 75 COOKIES

$^1/_2$	pound butter
$^1/_2$	cup brown sugar
$^1/_2$	cup white sugar
2	egg yolks
2	teaspoons vanilla extract
2	cups flour
	dash of salt
2	egg whites, slightly beaten
	pecan halves

Pecan Tea Cakes

❖ ❖ ❖

WHO DOESN'T LOVE THESE? THEY MELT IN YOUR MOUTH.

DOUGH:

4   ounces cream cheese

¹/₄ pound butter

1   cup flour

FILLING:

1   egg

    pinch of salt

1   teaspoon vanilla
    extract

³/₄ cup firmly packed
    brown sugar

1   tablespoon butter,
    melted

1   cup (or more) coarse-
    ly chopped nuts

Preheat oven to 375°F.

Blend cream cheese, butter, and flour. Refrigerate dough overnight. Shape dough into 24 1-inch balls. Press dough against bottom and up the sides of greased miniature muffin tins.

Beat together the filling ingredients.

Place half the nuts in the bottom of the shells. Spoon egg mixture over the nuts and top with remaining nuts.

Bake for 25 minutes, or until lightly browned. Allow to cool before gently removing from tins.

YIELD: 24 TEA CAKES

Powdered Meltaways

❖   ❖   ❖

AUNT ETHEL GAVE ME THIS RECIPE FIFTY-FIVE YEARS AGO.
THERE ARE MANY VERSIONS OF THIS, BUT THIS ONE IS MINE.
THE WHOLE FAMILY MAKES THESE. THEY DISAPPEAR QUICKLY.

Preheat oven to 400°F.

Blend the butter, sugar, and vanilla in a processor until creamy.
Add the flour and salt, which have been sifted together, and the
nuts. Process until smooth and soft.

Form dough into small balls and place on a cookie sheet lined
with baking parchment.

Bake for 8 minutes. While still warm, roll in powdered sugar.

$^1/_2$	pound butter
$^1/_2$	cup sifted powdered sugar
1	teaspoon vanilla extract
$2^1/_4$	cups sifted flour
$^1/_4$	teaspoon salt
1	cup ground pecans

VARIATION:

After making balls and placing them on cookie sheet, depress
each ball with a Hershey Chocolate Kiss. Bake as above, but
allow sufficient time for kiss to harden after removing from
oven. Do not roll in powdered sugar. I like to call them Dark
Persian Caps.

YIELD: 36 TO 48 COOKIES, DEPENDING UPON THE SIZE OF THE
BALLS

Sugar-Free Cookies

❖ ❖ ❖

AN EXCELLENT COOKIE FOR THOSE WHO MUST WATCH THEIR
SUGAR. FROM THE KITCHEN OF ARLENE GOLDBERG.

1³/₄	cups flour
2	teaspoons baking powder
¹/₂	teaspoon salt
¹/₂	teaspoon cinnamon
¹/₄	teaspoon cloves
¹/₈	teaspoon nutmeg
1	envelope Sweet 'n Low (do not use an aspartame product)
³/₄	cup orange juice
1	teaspoon grated fresh orange rind
¹/₂	scant cup oil
1	whole egg, or ¹/₄ cup egg substitute
1	cup chopped nuts
1	cup raisins

Preheat oven to 375°F.

Combine all the dry ingredients. Add the remaining ingredients and blend well.

Line a cookie sheet with baking parchment. Drop batter by tablespoon onto the cookie sheet, about 1 inch apart.

Bake for 15 to 20 minutes, until lightly brown. Cool on cookie sheet.

These freeze very well. Pop a couple in the microwave for about 50 seconds and enjoy.

YIELD: 18 TO 24 COOKIES

Toffee Squares

❖ ❖ ❖

THIS WAS, AND STILL IS, A FAMILY FAVORITE REQUESTED FOR
EVERY SWEET TABLE.

Preheat oven to 350°F.

Blend butter, sugar, and egg yolk until light and fluffy. Add vanilla, flour, and salt. Blend well.

Press dough into an ungreased jelly-roll pan. Bake for 15 to 20 minutes, until lightly browned.

While still hot, top with the melted chocolate chips, thinned with the 1/4 cup water. Top the chocolate with the ground nuts, pressing down slightly so that the nuts adhere to the chocolate.

Allow chocolate to harden before cutting. Placing the pan in the freezer for a few minutes may hasten the process.

YIELD: APPROXIMATELY 36 SQUARES

1/2 pound butter

1 cup brown sugar

1 egg yolk

1 teaspoon vanilla extract

2 cups flour

1/2 teaspoon salt

12 ounces semisweet chocolate chips, melted

1/4 cup water

1 cup ground pecans or walnuts

Non-Chocolate Toffee Cookie

❖   ❖   ❖

THIS WAS GRANDMA IDA'S VERSION OF THE TOFFEE COOKIE.
THIS RECIPE HAS TO BE AT LEAST SIXTY YEARS OLD. IT'S
DELICIOUS WITHOUT THE CHOCOLATE TOPPING.

¹/₂ pound	
1 cup brown sugar	
1 egg yolk	
1 teaspoon vanilla extract	
2 cups flour	
1 teaspoon cinnamon	
pinch of salt	
1 egg white, stiffly beaten	
1 cup chopped pecans or walnuts	

Preheat oven to 350°F.

Combine butter, sugar, egg yolk, and vanilla; beat until light and creamy. Add flour, cinnamon, and salt. Blend well.

Grease an 11 × 17-inch cookie sheet. Evenly spread the dough over the pan. With a pastry brush or large spoon, spread the beaten egg white over the dough. Sprinkle the nuts over the egg white and gently press down.

Bake for 25 to 30 minutes. Cut while warm.

YIELD: APPROXIMATELY 48 SQUARES

Chocolate Chip–Peanut Butter Cups

❖ ❖ ❖

A REAL WINNER WITH ALL AGES! SO SIMPLE TO MAKE.

Grease miniature muffin tins. Shape the dough into the size of a walnut and place in each space. Depress the dough so that it comes up around the sides.

Bake at 350°F for 10 to 12 minutes.

Remove from oven, and while still hot, place a Reese's Peanut Butter Cup over each cookie cup. Depress slightly. The heat from the cooky will melt the chocolate. Top with a white chocolate morsel.

Allow some time for these to harden. You can hasten the process by placing them on a flat surface in the freezer.

YIELD: 24 TO 30 CUPS

1 *roll of refrigerated Nestle's chocolate chip cookie dough*

Reese's miniature peanut butter cups (remove papers)

Nestle's white chocolate morsels

CAKE NOTES

Check your oven temperature from time to time, using an oven thermometer purchased in the kitchen section of your local hardware store.

From the standpoint of flavor, it is best to use butter when making cakes; however, half butter, half margarine may be used, or if you prefer, all margarine. The change should not alter the texture of your cake.

Under no circumstances should you use light butters or margarines. They contain too much liquid, and the results will not be satisfactory.

When sugar is called for, unless otherwise specified, it is always granulated sugar.

Confectioners' sugar and powdered sugar are one and the same.

I prefer using cake flour in most recipes. If you do not have it on hand, sift your regular flour several times, and then remeasure it.

Always use large or extra-large eggs.

When beating egg whites, always use a clean bowl and beaters. Egg whites should always be at room temperature. This will give you more volume.

Always grease and dust your pans lightly with flour, except for sponge cakes.

For those of you who have both a food processor and an electric mixer, please try to use your electric mixer when making a cake. Your cake will be lighter in texture. My daughters do not agree with me, but I feel very strongly about this. I couldn't manage without my food processor, but for cakes, stick with the mixer.

Most cakes can be frozen; however, slip them, uncovered, into the freezer for a few minutes. They will be easier to handle. Be sure to wrap them first in plastic wrap, then in aluminum foil, and then place them in a large plastic bag. By using plastic wrap first, you block out any odors that might exist from other items in the freezer.

When whipping cream for a frosting or topping, always place your bowl and beaters in the freezer for at least 30 minutes.

For the most satisfactory results, please follow the recipes carefully.

Chocolate Chip Cake

❖ ❖ ❖

THIS WAS ONE OF AUNT LILLIAN'S FAVORITE CAKES.

1	6-ounce package semisweet chocolate chips
1/4	cup water
2 1/4	cups cake flour
1	teaspoon baking soda
1/4	teaspoon salt
12	tablespoons butter or margarine
1 3/4	cups sugar
3	eggs
1	teaspoon vanilla extract
1	cup cold water

Preheat oven to 350°F.

Melt the chocolate chips with 1/4 cup water. Stir well and set aside.

Sift the cake flour, baking soda, and salt together and set aside.

Beat the butter or margarine and sugar until creamy. Add the eggs, one at a time, then the vanilla, and beat until thick and fluffy.

Add the melted chocolate and blend well.

Add the dry ingredients plus the 1 cup cold water and blend.

Grease a pan that is approximately 10 × 14 inches. Pour mixture into greased pan.

Bake for 35 to 40 minutes.

Insert toothpick in center of cake. If toothpick comes out clean, cake is ready to remove from the oven.

YIELD: **12 TO 16 SERVINGS**

German Chocolate Cake

❖   ❖   ❖

WHEN THIS RECIPE APPEARED ON THE SCENE MANY, MANY
YEARS AGO, IT WAS A SENSATION. IT HAS
REMAINED A FAVORITE.

Preheat oven to 350°F.

Melt chocolate in hot water; set aside.

Combine flour and salt. Set aside.

Add the baking soda to the buttermilk or sour cream and stir
well. Set aside.

Cream butter and sugar. Add vanilla and add eggs, one at a time,
and beat until light and creamy. Stir in the melted chocolate.

Add buttermilk mixture alternately with dry ingredients, beginning and ending with dry ingredients. Blend thoroughly after
each addition, using low speed on your electric mixer.

Turn into a greased and lightly floured 8-inch cake pan (or 9 ×
13-inch pan) and bake for 40 to 45 minutes.

Cool and frost with a chocolate frosting.

1	4-ounce bar Baker's German sweet choco- late
2	tablespoons hot water
2¼	cups sifted flour
1	teaspoon salt
1	teaspoon baking soda
1	cup buttermilk or sour cream
¼	pound butter
1¼	cups sugar
1	teaspoon vanilla extract
3	eggs

Flourless Chocolate Cake

❖　❖　❖

THIS CAKE MAY ALSO BE USED FOR PASSOVER INSTEAD OF
THE TRADITIONAL SPONGE CAKE.

5　very large eggs, sepa-
　rated (room tempera-
　ture)

²/₃　cup sugar

¼　pound unsalted but-
　ter (very soft)

4　ounces bittersweet or
　semisweet chocolate,
　melted and cooled

1　tablespoon Droste's
　cocoa

1　tablespoon dark rum

1　tablespoon coffee
　liqueur

1　tablespoon Droste's
　cocoa, for topping

Preheat oven to 325°F.

Place the egg yolks and ⅓ cup of sugar in a large bowl of the
electric mixer and beat on high speed until the mixture is very
thick and has increased in volume. Add the soft butter and continue to beat until batter is thick and smooth–3 to 4 minutes.
Add the chocolate and cocoa; mix well. Add rum and coffee
liqueur and blend. Set aside.

Using clean beaters and a clean bowl, beat the egg whites on
high speed until foamy. Gradually add the other ⅓ cup of
sugar, beating continually until the whites are thick and glossy.
Mix a quarter of the whites into the chocolate mixture; carefully *fold in* the remaining whites.

Grease an 8- or 9-inch springform pan and line the bottom with
baking parchment; grease the parchment.

Transfer batter to springform and bake for 45 to 60 minutes.
Test with a toothpick in the center of the cake. It should come
out clean.

Remove from oven and cool completely in the pan. (The cake
will sink in the center). Invert cake onto a serving plate and
remove the paper. Sift cocoa over the top.

YIELD: 8 TO 10 SERVINGS

French Pastry Chocolate Cake

❖ ❖ ❖

I REALLY THINK THIS IS ONE OF THE FINEST CHOCOLATE CAKES. IT IS SO LIGHT IN TEXTURE.

Preheat oven to 375°F.

Combine cocoa and boiling water. Set aside.

Combine sour cream and baking soda. Set aside.

Combine flour, salt, and baking powder. Set aside.

Beat the egg whites until thick and peaky.

Cream butter, sugar, and vanilla well. Add egg yolks, one at a time, and blend until creamy. Add cocoa mixture.

Add sour cream alternately with the dry ingredients, beginning and ending with the dry ingredients.

Lastly, fold in the beaten egg whites.

This can be made in layer cake pans or a 9 × 13-inch pan, lightly greased and floured.

Bake for 35 to 45 minutes. Test with a toothpick; when the toothpick comes out clean, the cake is done.

$^{1}/_{2}$ cup Droste's cocoa

$^{3}/_{4}$ cup boiling water

$^{1}/_{2}$ cup sour cream

$^{1}/_{2}$ teaspoon baking soda

2   cups sifted cake flour

$^{1}/_{2}$ teaspoon salt

$^{1}/_{2}$ teaspoon baking powder

3   eggs, separated (room temperature)

$^{1}/_{4}$ pound butter

2   cups sugar

1   teaspoon vanilla extract

Marble Cake

❖ ❖ ❖

THIS IS A TREASURED RECIPE FROM AUNT LOU, OUR DEAR
FRIEND, A MARVELOUS COOK, AND ALSO OUR NURSE WHEN
MANDY WAS BORN. FOR A LIGHTER CAKE,
USE YOUR ELECTRIC MIXER.

12   tablespoons butter

2¹/₂ cups cake flour

1¹/₂ teaspoon baking
      powder

1²/₃ cups sugar

1   cup sour cream

¹/₂   teaspoon baking
      soda

1   teaspoon vanilla
      extract

3   whole eggs

CHOCOLATE MIXTURE:

1   ounce unsweetened
      baking chocolate,
      melted

¹/₄   teaspoon baking
      soda

1   tablespoon sugar

2   tablespoons water

Cream the butter. Add the cake flour, baking powder, sugar, sour cream, baking soda, and vanilla extract. Beat for 2 minutes on low speed. Add the 3 whole eggs and beat again for 2 minutes on low speed.

Divide batter in half and add the chocolate mixture, which has been melted, to one half of the batter.

Pour the plain batter into a greased pan (approximately 9 × 13 inches) or two 9-inch layer pans. Using a large spoon, drop the chocolate mixture in rows onto the plain mixture; using a large fork, swirl the chocolate lightly through the plain batter.

Bake at 350°F for 30 minutes. Test with toothpick. When cool, frost with a chocolate frosting.

For a plain white cake: Reduce sugar to 1¹/₃ cups, and omit the chocolate mixture. I suggest frosting with my Broiled Brown Sugar Frosting.

Carrot Cake

❖ ❖ ❖

CARROT CAKES HAVE BECOME SO POPULAR. THIS IS
NOT AS RICH AS MOST. TRY IT.

Preheat oven to 325°F.

Sift the dry ingredients together. Set aside.

Cream the eggs, sugar, and oil until light and fluffy. Add the grated carrots; fold in the dry ingredients, together with the nuts.

Pour batter into a greased and floured pan, approximately 8½ × 11 inches.

Bake for 40 to 60 minutes.

When cool, frost with the following cream cheese frosting:

Blend the cream cheese and margarine until smooth and creamy. Add the vanilla and powdered sugar and beat until smooth.

YIELD: 12 SERVINGS

2	cups sifted cake flour
1	teaspoon baking powder
1	teaspoon baking soda
1	teaspoon salt
1	teaspoon cinnamon
½	teaspoon ground cloves
4	eggs
2	cups sugar
1	cup oil
3	cups grated carrots
½	cup chopped walnuts (optional)

CREAM CHEESE
FROSTING:

1	3-ounce package cream cheese
4	tablespoons margarine
1	teaspoon vanilla extract
2	cups sifted powdered sugar

Aunt Ida's Raisin Cake

❖ ❖ ❖

THIS WAS ALWAYS ONE OF AUNTIE IDA'S SPECIALTIES
AND IS A FAVORITE OF MANDY'S.

4   eggs

¹/₂ teaspoon salt

2   cups sugar

1   teaspoon vanilla
     extract

¹/₂ cup vegetable oil

2   cups bread flour

3   level teaspoons bak-
     ing powder

1   teaspoon cinnamon

¹/₂ teaspoon cloves

¹/₂ teaspoon nutmeg

1   box golden raisins

2   cups cold water

2   teaspoons baking
     soda

2   cups cake flour

1   cup chopped pecans

In a large electric mixer bowl, place the eggs and salt. Add the sugar and vanilla and blend well. Add the oil and blend well. Set aside.

Sift together the bread flour, baking powder, cinnamon, cloves, and nutmeg. Set aside.

Place the raisins in a saucepan. Add the cold water and bring to a boil. Add the baking soda and remove from heat. Allow to cool.

When ready preheat oven to 350°F. Add the egg and sugar mixture and the bread flour mixture to the mixing bowl. Blend. Add the following ingredients, blending after each one:

Add the cooled raisin mixture.

Add 1 cup of the cake flour.

Add the chopped pecans.

Add the last cup of cake flour.

Pour into a greased and lightly floured 9 × 13-inch pan and bake for 60 to 75 minutes. Test.

This cake is to be cut in slices as you would a pound cake. It is wonderful spread with cream cheese.

YIELD: AT LEAST 24 SLICES

White Delite Cake

❖   ❖   ❖

THIS IS A VERY NICE, EASY CAKE. NOT TOO RICH.

Preheat oven to 350°F.

In an electric mixer, cream butter and sugar until very light and creamy. Add flour, baking powder, sour cream, baking soda, and vanilla. Blend for 2 minutes on low speed.

Add the whole eggs and beat for another 2 minutes on low speed.

Pour into two 8-inch layer cake pans or a 9 × 13-inch loaf pan lightly greased and floured.

Bake for 30 minutes. Test. Remove from oven when done.

If making a 9 × 13-inch loaf, spread with Broiled Brown Sugar Frosting. Return to oven until it bubbles.

If using layer cake pans, use the Cream Cheese Frosting or any chocolate frosting.

12	tablespoons butter
$1^1/_3$	cups sugar
$2^1/_2$	cups cake flour
$1^1/_2$	teaspoons baking powder
1	cup sour cream
$^1/_2$	teaspoon baking soda
1	teaspoon vanilla extract
3	whole eggs

Poppy Seed Cake

❖ ❖ ❖

I RECEIVED THIS RECIPE FROM MY DEAR FRIEND,
SALLY ARIES, MANY YEARS AGO.

¹/₂	cup poppy seeds
1	cup milk
¹/₄	pound butter
1¹/₂	cups sugar
¹/₈	teaspoon salt
1	teaspoon vanilla extract
2	cups cake flour
2	teaspoons baking powder
4	egg whites, stiffly beaten

Soak the poppy seeds in the milk for 2 hours.

Preheat oven to 350°F.

Cream butter and sugar together thoroughly. Add the poppy seed mixture, salt, and vanilla. Add flour and baking powder, which have been sifted together. Fold in the beaten egg whites.

Pour into a well-greased 9- or 10-inch tube pan.

Bake for 1 hour.

When cool, dust with powdered sugar.

YIELD: 8 TO 10 SERVINGS

California Coffee Cake

❖ ❖ ❖

SOUR CREAM COFFEE CAKES BECAME VERY POPULAR ABOUT FIFTY YEARS AGO, ONLY WE CALLED THEM CALIFORNIA COFFEE CAKES. THEY ARE SERVED AS OFTEN TODAY AS THEY WERE YEARS AGO.

Preheat oven to 350°F. Grease a 9-inch tube pan with removable bottom and lightly dust with flour.

Combine the flour, baking powder, and salt. Set aside.

Combine sour cream and baking soda. Set aside.

Combine the chopped nuts, sugar, and cinnamon for the topping. Set aside.

Combine butter, eggs, sugar, and extracts and beat until very light and fluffy. Add sour cream and baking soda mixture. Blend well.

Incorporate the flour mixture.

Pour half of the batter into the tube pan. Top with half of the topping mixture. Cover with the remaining batter and the balance of the topping mixture.

Bake for 45 to 60 minutes. When cool, remove from pan.

YIELD: 8 TO 10 SERVINGS

2   cups flour

1   teaspoon baking powder

$^{1}/_{8}$ teaspoon salt

1   cup sour cream

1   teaspoon baking soda

$^{1}/_{4}$ pound butter

2   eggs

1   cup sugar

$^{1}/_{4}$ teaspoon almond extract

$^{1}/_{4}$ teaspoon lemon extract

$^{1}/_{2}$ teaspoon vanilla extract

TOPPING:

$^{1}/_{2}$ cup chopped nuts

$^{1}/_{2}$ cup sugar

1   tablespoon cinnamon

Apple Pound Cake

❖ ❖ ❖

MY FAMILY LOVES ANYTHING MADE WITH APPLES. THIS IS A GREAT CAKE!

3	cups unsifted flour
1	teaspoon baking soda
1	teaspoon salt
1	teaspoon cinnamon
1/2	teaspoon nutmeg
1/2	teaspoon ground cloves
1 1/2	cups vegetable oil
2	cups sugar
3	eggs
2	teaspoons vanilla extract
2	cups pared and finely chopped apples (McIntosh or Granny Smith)
1	cup chopped pecans
1/2	cup raisins

Preheat oven to 325°F.

Combine flour, baking soda, salt, and spices; set aside.

In large bowl of electric mixer, at medium speed, beat together oil, sugar, eggs, and vanilla until thoroughly combined.

Gradually fold in flour mixture until smooth. Fold in apples, pecans, and raisins.

Turn into a greased and floured 10-inch tube pan with removable bottom.

Bake for 1 hour and 15 minutes, or until cake tester inserted near center comes out clean.

Cool cake in pan, on a wire rack, for 10 minutes. Remove from pan, and after cake has completely cooled, store in airtight container.

Freezes well.

YIELD: 12 TO 18 SLICES

Orange-Walnut Cake

❖　❖　❖

THIS WAS ALWAYS ONE OF MY FAVORITES. IT IS WONDERFUL!
I HAVE HAD THIS RECIPE FOR AT LEAST FIFTY YEARS.
THANK YOU, AUNT ETHEL.

Preheat oven to 350°F.

Combine cake flour, salt, and baking powder. Set aside.
Combine baking soda and buttermilk. Set aside.

Cream butter, sugar, eggs, and vanilla until light and creamy.

Alternately add flour mixture and buttermilk mixture, beginning and ending with the flour mixture.

Add the grated rind and the chopped walnuts.

Turn into a greased and lightly floured 9-inch square pan. Bake for 40 to 45 minutes.

Bring syrup ingredients to a boil. When cake is partially cool, immediately pour hot syrup over cake.

YIELD: 8 TO 10 SERVINGS

12	tablespoons butter
1	cup sugar
2	eggs (room temperature)
2½	cups cake flour
¼	teaspoon salt
2	teaspoons baking powder
1½	teaspoon baking soda
1	cup buttermilk
	grated rind of 2 navel oranges (save oranges for syrup)
1	cup chopped walnuts
1	teaspoon vanilla extract

SYRUP:

| | juice from 2 oranges and ½ lemon |
| 1 | cup sugar |

Chocolate Cheesecake

❖   ❖   ❖

**THIS IS ABSOLUTELY SCRUMPTIOUS. FROM THE KITCHEN
OF MY DAUGHTER, MARSHA.**

CRUST:

¹/₄   cup flour

¹/₄   cup brown sugar

¹/₄   pound butter

¹/₂   cup chopped nuts

FILLING:

*2   8-ounce packages
cream cheese*

3   egg yolks

³/₄   cup sugar

*1   teaspoon vanilla
extract*

*3   egg whites, beaten
until stiff and peaky*

*³/₄   cup chocolate chips,
melted with 3 table-
spoons milk*

TOPPING:

1¹/₂ cups sour cream

*1   teaspoon vanilla
extract*

2   tablespoons sugar

Combine the crust ingredients and press gently into a 9 × 13-inch greased pan. Bake at 350°F for 15 minutes, until light brown.

Cream the cheese. Add egg yolks, one at a time. Gradually add sugar. Add the vanilla. Blend well. Fold the beaten whites into the cream cheese mixture. Pour over the baked crust. Drizzle the melted chocolate over the cake and swirl with a fork.

Bake at 350°F for 20 to 25 minutes. Remove from oven.

Combine the topping ingredients and spread over the baked cheesecake. Return to oven and bake at 350° for an additional 8 minutes, or until top begins to crack.

This is a very high cake. Should you desire to use a larger pan, I would suggest you cut the baking time.

This freezes very well. Cover with plastic wrap first, and then with aluminum foil.

YIELD: AT LEAST 12 TO 18 SERVINGS

Spiced Pumpkin Cheesecake

❖　❖　❖

THIS IS ANOTHER DELICIOUS THANKSGIVING DESSERT.

Preheat oven to 350°F.

In a food processor, blend cream cheese and sugars until fluffy. Add eggs and blend. Add remaining ingredients and blend well.

Pour into a 10-inch springform pan. Bake for 80 minutes. Turn off oven. Allow cake to cool in oven. Refrigerate overnight.

To serve, remove springform ring and garnish with whipped cream.

This can be frozen, uncovered, and then removed from the springform bottom. Wrap carefully and place back in freezer.

3	8-ounce packages cream cheese
³/₄	cup white sugar
³/₄	cup brown sugar (solidly packed)
4	eggs
1	16-ounce can pumpkin
1¹/₄	teaspoon ground cinnamon
¹/₂	teaspoon ground nutmeg
¹/₄	teaspoon ground cloves
1	teaspoon vanilla extract

Combine all ingredients and press firmly into bottom and halfway up the sides of your 10-inch springform pan. Now, add your filling.

OPTIONAL CRUST:

1¹/₄	cups graham cracker crumbs
¹/₂	cup finely chopped walnuts
¹/₄	cup sugar
5	tablespoons margarine, melted
¹/₂	teaspoon ground nutmeg

YIELD: 12 TO 18 SERVINGS

Kahlúa Cheesecake

❖ ❖ ❖

THIS RECIPE ORIGINALLY CAME FROM A CHICAGO
RESTAURANT. IT HAS ALWAYS BEEN MY
FAVORITE CHEESECAKE.

1	pound cottage cheese
1¹/₂	pounds cream cheese
1³/₄	cups sugar
5	eggs
1	teaspoon vanilla extract
2	cups sour cream
³/₄	cup butter or margarine, melted
¹/₄	cup flour
¹/₄	cup cornstarch
4	tablespoons Droste's cocoa
¹/₃	to ¹/₂ cup Kahlúa liqueur

Preheat oven to 350°F.

In a processor, combine cheeses and beat until thoroughly creamed. Add sugar, eggs, and vanilla and blend well. Add sour cream and melted butter and blend. Incorporate flour and cornstarch.

Pour into a well-greased 9-inch springform pan, reserving about ¹/₂ cup.

Mix cocoa with Kahlúa; add to the reserved ¹/₂ cup of batter. Swirl cocoa and Kahlúa mixture into batter in springform.

Bake for 70 minutes.

Cool in oven for several hours without opening oven door.

Chill cake until firm. This also freezes beautifully.

Note: To reduce the fat content of this recipe, low-fat cheeses and light or fat-free sour cream may be substituted.

YIELD: 12 TO 18 SERVINGS

Ice Cream Cake and Topping

❖　❖　❖

BEFORE THE "CHOLESTEROL" ERA, I MADE THIS ALL THE TIME. THIS WAS ALWAYS A BIG HIT. IT NOT ONLY TASTED GOOD, BUT IT LOOKED BEAUTIFUL. USE AT LEAST THREE FLAVORS OF ICE CREAM AND TAKE COLOR INTO CONSIDERATION.

Line a 9- or 10-inch springform with the ladyfingers, around the side and on the bottom. You can piece the bottom, if necessary. Spread the softened ice cream as quickly as you can, packing it down, first one layer and then another.

Cover with plastic wrap and put in freezer at once.

Heat topping ingredients over moderate to high heat, stirring constantly, until almost candied. Using a fork, spread immediately over frozen cake, until top is completely covered.

Wrap tightly in plastic wrap and then in foil. Place in a plastic bag and return to freezer. Remove from freezer about 30 minutes before serving.

This dessert will keep in the freezer for several weeks.

Note: Should you need the springform pan for another use, freeze the cake thoroughly. Remove it from the form, using a flat knife to remove it from the bottom. Proceed with the wrapping as described above.

YIELD: 12 TO 18 SLICES

2　*packages of lady-fingers, separated*

3　*varieties of ice cream (quantity needed will depend upon the quality of the ice cream; allow ice cream to soften slightly, to enable you to spread it in layers)*

TOPPING:

6　*tablespoons butter or margarine*

¹/₂　cup sugar

2　*cups chopped pecans or sliced almonds*

Honey Cake (Lekach)

❖ ❖ ❖

**THERE IS NOTHING LIKE A HONEY CAKE FOR A
SWEET NEW YEAR.**

¹/₂ cup raisins	Combine raisins and brandy in a saucepan and simmer until brandy is absorbed. Set aside.
2 tablespoons brandy	
3¹/₄ cups sifted cake flour	
1¹/₂ teaspoons baking powder	Sift flour, baking powder, baking soda, allspice, cinnamon, and cloves together and set aside.
¹/₂ teaspoon baking soda	
¹/₂ teaspoon allspice	Beat egg whites until fluffy and add apple juice concentrate, honey, and vanilla. Beat until thick and soft peaks form, 10 to 12 minutes.
¹/₂ teaspoon cinnamon	
¹/₄ teaspoon ground cloves	
5 extra-large egg whites (room temperature)	Mix raisins, walnuts and flour mixture together. Fold into the egg white mixture and mix thoroughly.
1 cup frozen apple juice concentrate, thawed	Preheat oven to 325°F.

Line a 10-inch tube pan with waxed paper or baking parchment. |
¹/₂ cup honey	
1 teaspoon vanilla extract	Pour batter into tube pan and bake for 45 minutes.
¹/₂ cup chopped walnuts	Remove pan from oven, invert, and cool completely.

YIELD: 12 SLICES

Chocolate Cupcakes

❖   ❖   ❖

THIS WAS ALWAYS A FAVORITE WITH MY CHILDREN WHEN
THEY WERE YOUNG, ESPECIALLY AT BIRTHDAY PARTIES; ONE
OF THE MOST SUCCESSFUL ACTIVITIES AT A PARTY WAS TO
LET THE LITTLE GUESTS DO THEIR OWN FROSTING
AND DECORATING.

Preheat oven to 350°F.

Melt the chocolate and set aside.

Sift flour with a dash of salt. Set aside.

Add the baking soda to the sour cream. Stir well. It will rise and get foamy. Set aside.

Cream butter and sugar together. Add eggs and beat until light and fluffy. Add melted chocolate and the vanilla. Add the sour cream and flour alternately, ending with the flour. Blend well, but be careful not to overbeat.

Pour into greased muffin tins and bake for 15 to 20 minutes.

Frost with one of my chocolate frostings.

YIELD: 12 CUPCAKES

2	squares unsweetened baking chocolate
2	cups cake flour
$^1/_8$	teaspoon salt
1	teaspoon baking soda
1	cup sour cream
$^1/_4$	pound butter
1	cup sugar
2	eggs
1	teaspoon vanilla extract

Basic Chocolate Frosting

❖ ❖ ❖

VERY BASIC, BUT DELICIOUS.

1	ounce unsweetened baking chocolate
2	tablespoons butter
1¹/₂	cups powdered sugar
1	tablespoon hot water
¹/₂	teaspoon vanilla extract

Melt the chocolate and butter.

Add sugar, hot water, and vanilla. Beat until smooth. If too thick, adjust with a little more hot water.

For a mocha flavor, use strong coffee instead of water.

YIELD: COVERS 18 SQUARE INCHES

Glossy Chocolate Icing

❖ ❖ ❖

DRIZZLE THIS OVER BROWNIES OR ANY CHOCOLATE CAKE.

3	tablespoons hot milk
2	tablespoons soft butter
2	cups powdered sugar, sifted
1	teaspoon vanilla extract
2	ounces unsweetened baking chocolate, melted

Combine hot milk and butter. Add sifted sugar and vanilla. Beat until smooth.

Add melted chocolate and mix well. If too thick, add a little more hot milk. If a coffee-flavored frosting is desired, substitute hot coffee for the milk.

YIELD: ENOUGH FROSTING FOR A BATCH OF BROWNIES OR A LARGE CAKE

Chocolate Whipped Cream Frosting

❖ ❖ ❖

A GREAT WAY TO DRESS UP A SPONGE CAKE.

Mix all the ingredients together in a large electric mixer bowl. Chill in refrigerator for 2 hours.

Place your beaters for mixer in freezer.

Remove after 2 hours, and whip mixture until stiff.

After frosting cake, place it in the refrigerator until ready to serve.

6 tablespoons Droste's cocoa

1 cup sugar

2 cups whipping cream

   pinch of salt

YIELD: ENOUGH FROSTING TO FILL AND FROST 1 9-INCH SPONGE CAKE CUT INTO 3 LAYERS

Broiled Brown Sugar Frosting

❖　❖　❖

ONE OF MY VERY FAVORITE TOPPINGS FOR ANY WHITE CAKE.

2　tablespoons soft
　　butter

¹/₃　cup soft brown sugar

³/₄　cup finely chopped
　　nuts or coconut

3　tablespoons cream

Combine butter with brown sugar. Cook over a low flame until melted. Add nuts or coconut, alternately with cream, making a proper consistency to spread.

Spread over warm cake.

Broil at 325°F about 1 inch from the heat, until bubbles form and it browns. Watch carefully that it does not burn.

Cream Cheese Frosting

❖　❖　❖

GOOD ON ANY WHITE CAKE, BUT A MUST FOR A CARROT CAKE.

1　3-ounce package
　　cream cheese

1　tablespoon orange
　　juice

¹/₂　teaspoon grated
　　orange rind

2¹/₂　cups powdered sugar

Blend together cream cheese, orange juice, and rind. Add sugar gradually, mixing until thick and creamy.

YIELD: ENOUGH FROSTING FOR 16 TO 18 CUPCAKES OR THE TOP OF A 9 × 13-INCH LOAF CAKE

Mocha Frosting

❖ ❖ ❖

I HAVE ALWAYS LIKED THE COMBINATION OF COFFEE
AND CHOCOLATE.

Cream butter. Add cocoa, instant coffee, vanilla, salt, and hot milk.

Add sugar, blending until thick and creamy. If too thick, add a little more hot milk. For a stronger coffee flavor, add a little more instant coffee.

YIELD: ENOUGH FROSTING FOR 1 CAKE

6 to 8 tablespoons butter

$^1/_4$ cup Droste's cocoa

1 teaspoon instant coffee powder

1 teaspoon vanilla extract

$^1/_4$ teaspoon salt

7 to 8 tablespoons hot milk

$4^1/_4$ cups powdered sugar

Boiled Icing

❖ ❖ ❖

A LITTLE TRICKY TO MAKE. TAKE YOUR TIME, BECAUSE IT IS A
BEAUTIFUL, PEAKY ICING.

In a large electric mixer bowl, beat egg whites until slightly foamy. Add the salt and beat until stiff and peaky. Set aside.

In a large saucepan, mix the balance of the ingredients. Cook over low heat, until very thick and it "beads up" in cold water.

Remove from heat and fold into the beaten egg whites.

YIELD: WILL FROST A 10-INCH SPONGE CAKE

2 egg whites

$^1/_4$ teaspoon salt

$2^1/_4$ cups sugar

$^1/_2$ cup light corn syrup

$^1/_2$ cup water

1 teaspoon vanilla extract

Fruit Tart

❖　❖　❖

I BELIEVE THIS WAS BONNIE RUBIN'S RECIPE. WHEN WE
WERE COMING FOR DINNER, SHE ALWAYS MADE IT WITH MY
HUSBAND'S FAVORITE BLUEBERRY FILLING. MARVELOUS!

CRUST:

1	cup walnuts or pecans
¼	pound unsalted butter
3	tablespoons sugar
1½	cups flour
½	teaspoon vanilla extract
1	egg yolk

FILLING:

Strawberries, blue-
berries, and/or kiwi,
or a combination

GLAZE:

2	envelopes Knox gelatin
2	tablespoons brandy or liqueur
1	10- to 12-ounce jar currant jelly

Place all the ingredients for the crust in a food processor.
Incorporate until just blended. Press into a 10-inch tart pan.
Chill for 1 hour. Preheat oven to 400°F. Bake for 20 to 30 min-
utes, or until crust begins to brown.

To make the glaze, place the gelatin and brandy in a saucepan.
Let soften for 1 minute and add the currant jelly. Stir over low
heat until smooth. Cool slightly. When the crust is cool, fill with
the fruit and cover with glaze. Allow to set.

YIELD: 8 TO 10 SERVINGS

Cream Cheese Filling (optional)

❖ ❖ ❖

YOU MIGHT LIKE THIS TYPE OF FILLING FOR YOUR
FRUIT TART.

Combine all the ingredients until smooth and creamy.

Spread on the bottom of the fruit tart crust, then add the fruit and glaze.

1 8-ounce package cream cheese

4 tablespoons sugar

1 egg

$^1/_2$ teaspoon vanilla extract

$^1/_2$ teaspoon lemon juice

Pecan Pie

❖   ❖   ❖

CALORIES DON'T COUNT. JUST ENJOY!

Preheat oven to 350°F.	1 9-inch pastry shell, unbaked
	3 eggs, slightly beaten
Mix eggs, corn syrup, sugar, butter, and vanilla until well blended.	1 cup light or dark corn syrup
	1 cup sugar
Cover the unbaked pie crust with the pecans. Pour the egg mixture over the pecans.	2 tablespoons butter, melted
Bake for 50 to 55 minutes, or until a knife inserted halfway between center and edge comes out clean.	1 teaspoon vanilla extract
	1½ cups pecan halves
Cool. Serve with whipped cream.	

YIELD: 8 SERVINGS

Pecan Tart

❖ ❖ ❖

MY DAUGHTER, JOANNE GIMBEL, ALWAYS MAKES THIS FOR
ME. IT'S MY SPECIAL TREAT! I JUST THROW CAUTION TO
THE WINDS.

Preheat oven to 350°F. Blend the pastry ingredients well in a
food processor and press into an 8-inch tart pan.

For the filling, blend sugar and butter until fluffy. Add eggs,
syrup, vanilla, and salt and blend well.

Sprinkle chopped pecans over pastry shell. Pour one half of the
filling over the nuts. Place pecan halves over filling and gently
spoon balance of filling over pecan halves.

Bake for 60 to 70 minutes.

Cool completely before removing outer rim from tart pan.

A little whipped cream can't hurt!

YIELD: 8 SERVINGS

PASTRY:

1	cup flour
1/3	cup powdered sugar
12	tablespoons butter
1/8	teaspoon salt

FILLING:

3/4	cup brown sugar
3	tablespoons butter
3	eggs
3/4	cup dark corn syrup
2	teaspoons vanilla extract
1/8	teaspoon salt
2	cups chopped pecans
1 1/2	cups pecan halves

Kuchen Dough

❖   ❖   ❖

THIS IS A EUROPEAN TYPE OF PASTRY DOUGH. JUST LIKE
GRANDMA USED TO MAKE.

1½ cups flour

¼ cup sugar

½ teaspoon baking
powder

12 tablespoons butter

3 tablespoons orange
juice

1 teaspoon vanilla
extract

Preheat oven to 425°F.

Place all the ingredients in a food processor and process until it
forms a ball. Remove from processor, wrap in waxed paper, and
refrigerate for at least 1 hour.

Place the dough in a 10-inch deep-dish pie plate or a 10-inch
tart pan. Pat into place. Crimp edges if using pie plate. Line the
pan with foil and weight down with uncooked beans, such as
lima beans.

Place in oven and bake on lowest rack for about 10 minutes.
Reduce oven heat to 375°F. Bake until the crust is lightly brown
on the bottom, about 5 minutes. Remove from the oven and
carefully remove the foil and beans.

This is a marvelous crust for a fresh fruit tart or any filling that
does not require additional baking.

See following recipes for filling and topping.

Fruit Kuchens

❖ ❖ ❖

WHEN FRUITS WERE IN SEASON, I ALWAYS MADE SEVERAL
KUCHENS AND FROZE THEM UNBAKED. OF COURSE, THIS
MEANT PURCHASING A SUPPLY OF PANS. THERE IS
SOMETHING SPECIAL ABOUT SERVING A FRUIT TART WHEN
THE FRUIT IS OUT OF SEASON.

KUCHEN DOUGH: SEE PRECEDING RECIPE AND PROCEED
ACCORDING TO DIRECTIONS. FOR A FRESH FRUIT TART THAT
DOES NOT REQUIRE ADDITIONAL BAKING, PLEASE REFER TO
MY "FRUIT TART" IN THIS SECTION; HOWEVER, IF MAKING A
FRESH APPLE, PEACH, OR PLUM KUCHEN, DO NOT PREBAKE
THE CRUST. SPRINKLE THE BOTTOM OF THE CRUST WITH
STREUSEL TOPPING (SEE FOLLOWING RECIPE), THEN FILL.

If you are using a smaller pan, adjust the quantity needed.

Toss the fruit with the fresh lemon juice. Then toss with the
sugar and flour to coat well.

Arrange the fruit in the pastry crust spiral pattern.

Cover generously with the Streusel Topping.

Bake at 350°F for 45 minutes, or until crust is browned.

A tart can be frozen raw, and baked at a later date. Allow a little more time for baking.

FILLING:

fresh fruit of your choice

$^1/_3$ cup fresh lemon juice

$^1/_4$ cup sugar

$^1/_4$ cup flour

FOR A 10-INCH TART
PAN, USE:

8 to 10 large peaches,
peeled and sliced

8 to 10 McIntosh or
Granny Smith apples,
peeled and sliced

FOR A 12-INCH TART
PAN OR 10-INCH
SPRINGFORM, USE:

2 to 3 pounds pitted
Italian plums

Streusel Topping for Fruit Kuchens

❖ ❖ ❖

I SUGGEST YOU DOUBLE OR TRIPLE THIS RECIPE SO
YOU ALWAYS HAVE IT ON HAND. IT WILL KEEP IN
THE REFRIGERATOR.

³/₄ cup sugar

3   tablespoons flour

2   tablespoons butter

¹/₈ teaspoon nutmeg for
a peach kuchen

¹/₂ teaspoon cinnamon
for apple or plum
kuchens

Blend in a food processor until crumbly.

Pumpkin Pie

❖ ❖ ❖

THIS TYPE OF PUMPKIN PIE HAS ALWAYS BEEN MY FAVORITE
DESSERT AT THANKSGIVING.

Preheat oven to 425°F.

Mix eggs, pumpkin, and sugar. Blend well. Add salt and spices
and blend once again. Blend in the evaporated milk.

Pour into unbaked pie shell. Bake for 15 minutes. Reduce oven
temperature to 350°F and continue baking for 45 minutes, or
until a toothpick inserted in center of pie filling comes out
clean.

Remove from oven and cool on a rack.

Serve with whipped cream or my Crunchy Pecan Topping (see
following recipe).

2	eggs (slightly beaten)
1	1-pound can solid-pack pumpkin
3/4	cup sugar
1/2	teaspoon salt
1	teaspoon cinnamon
1/2	teaspoon cloves
1/2	teaspoon ginger
1 2/3	cups evaporated milk
1	9-inch unbaked pie shell with high fluted edge*

*If using regular frozen pie shells, this recipe will fill two. Place on a cook-
ie sheet in a preheated 425°F oven for 15 minutes. Reduce heat to 350°F, and
continue baking for about 30 minutes, or until pies test done with toothpick
inserted as above.

If using deep-dish frozen pie shells, recipe fills one. Let shell thaw for 10
minutes; crimp edge so that it stands ¹/₂ inch above rim of pie plate. Bake
on a cookie sheet in preheated 425°F oven for 15 minutes. Reduce heat to
350°F, and continue baking for about 50 minutes, or until pie tests done, as
noted above.

Crunchy Pecan Topping

❖ ❖ ❖

THIS REALLY PUTS THE FINISHING TOUCH ON A PUMPKIN PIE.

1 cup coarsely chopped
   pecans

²/₃ cup firmly packed
   light brown sugar

1 tablespoon butter,
   melted

Mix the pecans and brown sugar together. Drizzle the melted butter over and stir until completely moistened.

Sprinkle this over a cooled pumpkin pie.

Place under the broiler about 5 inches from heat and broil for 1 to 2 minutes, or until topping is bubbly. This may be served warm, or allow to cool and serve with whipped cream or a dairy topping.

Passover

OUR PASSOVER

Memories of Passover seders in the Patinkin family are something every member of the family will cherish.

My mother-in-law, Grandma Celia, was our hostess, but Aunties Ida and Lillian did all the preparation. The seders were always held at Auntie Ida's and Uncle Harold Dray's home, inasmuch as they were the only ones who "kashered" their home for Passover.

Now, Grandma Celia and Grandpa Max (he died before Mandy was born) had four children: Lillian, Ida, Lester, and Harold (referred to as Uncle Schmule). Each one was married: Lillian to Sol Levine, Ida to Harold Dray, Lester to Doralee Patinkin, and Harold to June Patinkin. So there we had eight people, plus Grandma Celia, who lived with Auntie Ida. Now we are up to nine. The four children and their spouses produced fourteen grandchildren. Now we are up to twenty-three people! This was the minimum number present when we were all young. Some of the older grandchildren married, and if they were in town they were there with their spouses.

There were tables in every room, but everyone crowded around the main table for the reading of the Haggadah. There was always a great deal of music, and as the kids became older, they "rocked" a bit. Mandy's father, Lester, always hid the Afikomen. It was a memorable time.

The table was always beautiful, set with Auntie Ida's red glass plates, used only for Passover. The food was fabulous, the desserts were bountiful, and someone always found the Afikomen. The winner was well compensated. All the others always received a lesser amount.

The second Passover seder was always celebrated with my side of the family at our home. I would pull out all the stops. Everything was pretty much the same as the first night, except for the fewer number of youngsters present.

The passage of time changes many things. Grandma Celia, Lester, Lillian, and Sol have died; all our children married, had their own children, and some moved out of Chicago. They all celebrate Passover.

In 1974 I remarried, to Stanley Rubin, and ten years later moved to San Diego. I am fortunate to have two daughters living in San Diego, mine, Marsha Patinkin, and my husband's, Joanne Gimbel.

We carry on the tradition of beautiful seders in San Diego, usually at the Gimbels' home, where recently the grandchildren have started to conduct the seder.

Occasionally, I have gone to Marsha's home (when she lived in Reno) and to Mandy and Kathryn's in New York for Passover.

Our children and grandchildren have picked up the gauntlet and the tradition of Passover is observed with beauty and dignity in all their homes.

The following Passover recipes are a few traditional ones. Be creative. Many of your regular recipes can be adapted for Passover very easily.

I sincerely hope you have a Passover holiday as beautiful as ours have always been and, I hope, will continue to be.

Charoses

❖ ❖ ❖

THIS DELICIOUS CONCOCTION IS ONE OF THE SYMBOLIC
FOODS PLACED ON THE SEDER PLATE. ITS MEANING IS
DESCRIBED DURING THE READING OF THE HAGGADAH ON
PASSOVER. IT IS LOVED BY EVERYONE; HUGE QUANTITIES ARE
ALWAYS MADE TO BE EATEN DURING THE SEDER, OR ANY
LEFTOVERS, DURING THE WEEK OF PASSOVER. THERE ARE
MANY, MANY RECIPES FOR CHAROSES. THIS IS MY FAMILY'S
RECIPE. BEFORE FOOD PROCESSORS ARRIVED ON THE SCENE,
WE USED AN OLD-FASHIONED CHOPPING BOWL AND
METAL CHOPPER.

Core the apples and cut into chunks. Place all the ingredients in a food processor. Using the steel blade, pulse on and off. You do not want the mixture to become watery. It should be mildly coarse, resembling mortar, which it represents on the seder plate. Should you have a problem, add more ground nuts. By the way, *I* never use the honey.

YIELD: 18 SERVINGS

12	large McIntosh apples
3	cups pecans
$^1/_2$	cup Concord grape or Malaga wine
$1^1/_2$	tablespoons ground cinnamon
$^1/_2$	teaspoon ground cloves
$^1/_2$	teaspoon ground ginger
$1^1/_2$	tablespoons honey (optional)

SPONGE CAKE NOTES

As a young bride, I knew nothing about making sponge cakes. Auntie Ida taught me everything. I used to "knock out" several at one time and freeze them; however, one time when I was in Reno, where my daughter lived at that time, I started to bake. The winds were extremely high in Reno that night. That, coupled with the higher altitude, caused one disaster after another. After three cakes completely collapsed, I stopped. The next morning the winds had died down and I proceeded as usual. Every cake was perfect. By the way, should you have a cake collapse, cut it up and toast it as you would mandelbrot; if you make a trifle, as my daughter Marsha does, freeze the cut-up pieces. I never throw anything away if I can salvage it.

Use an electric mixer–do not use a food processor.

Use extra-large eggs.

Separate the eggs and allow them to stand at room temperature for at least 30 minutes.

Always beat the egg whites with a pinch of salt until foamy, and then add a little of the sugar before beating into stiff peaks.

Beat the egg yolks, sugar, and liquid until thick and creamy.

Add the cake meal to the yolk mixture and blend.

Fold the yolk and cake meal mixture into the beaten whites.

Always use a tube pan or a springform pan with removable bottoms.

Do not grease the pan.

After pouring the batter into the pan, be sure to plunge your spatula, knife, or fork around the batter.

Bake on the lower rack in your oven.

Always test to see if done before removing from oven.

Always invert cake–either on a counter if your pan has prongs, or insert a bottle into the tube of your pan, and let the cake hang upside down. If using a springform, invert on a cake rack. Allow several hours for cooling and stretching.

Run a knife around the sides of the pan, trying not to break into the sides of the cake.

Remove the cake carefully.

Sponge cakes freeze very well. Remove the cake from the pan, wrap it very loosely in waxed paper, and then cover with foil; place in a large plastic bag and freeze.

Passover Chocolate Sponge Cake

❖   ❖   ❖

MY CHILDREN ALWAYS PREFERRED THIS CAKE. IT'S GREAT
WITH A FRUIT SAUCE OR MY RASPBERRY FLUFF, AND
WHIPPED CREAM OR DAIRY TOPPING.

¹/₄ cup Droste's cocoa

³/₄ cup cake meal

¹/₃ cup potato starch

¹/₈ teaspoon salt

*10   extra-large eggs, sepa-
rated*

2   cups sugar

*1   navel orange, juice
and grated rind*

YIELD: 12 TO 14

SLICES

Sift the dry ingredients and set aside.

Preheat oven to 350°F.

Using an electric mixer, beat the yolks until thick. Add 1 cup of
the sugar, the juice, and orange rind. Continue beating until
thick and fluffy. Fold in dry ingredients.

In a separate bowl, beat egg whites and a pinch of salt until
foamy. Add the other 1 cup of sugar gradually. Beat until stiff
peaks form.

Fold egg yolk mixture into egg whites.

Pour into an ungreased 10-inch tube pan with a removable bottom. Plunge a spatula or fork around the batter several times to
equalize it.

Bake on the low rack of the oven for 60 minutes. Test with a
toothpick. Insert into cake; if it comes out clean, your cake is
ready to remove from the oven.

Invert for several hours to cool and stretch.

This cake may be frozen.

Passover Sponge Cake 1

❖　❖　❖

THIS IS ONE VERSION OF THE "TRADITIONAL" SPONGE CAKE.
IT IS WONDERFUL SERVED WITH MY LEMON FLUFF. WHEN
MANDY WAS A LITTLE BOY, THIS WAS ONE OF HIS FAVORITE
PASSOVER DESSERTS.

Preheat oven to 325°F.

Sift the dry ingredients and set aside.

Using an electric mixer, beat the egg yolks until thick. Add $1/2$ cup of the sugar, lemon juice, and orange rind. Continue beating until thick and fluffy. Fold in dry ingredients.

In a separate bowl, beat the egg whites and a pinch of salt until foamy. Add the other $1/2$ cup of sugar gradually. Beat until stiff peaks form.

Fold egg yolk mixture into egg whites.

Pour into an ungreased 10-inch tube pan. Bake for 45 to 50 minutes. Test with a toothpick. Insert into cake; if it comes out clean, your cake is ready to remove from the oven.

Invert pan for several hours so cake can cool and stretch.

This cake may be frozen.

YIELD: 12 TO 14 SLICES

$1/3$ cup cake meal

$1/2$ cup potato starch

$1/8$ teaspoon salt

10　extra-large eggs, separated

1　cup sugar

　　juice of 1 lemon (just under $1/4$ cup)

　　grated rind of 1 navel orange

Passover Sponge Cake 2

❖   ❖   ❖

THIS IS ANOTHER VERSION OF THE "TRADITIONAL" SPONGE
CAKE. SLIGHTLY SMALLER. SERVE WITH MY LEMON FLUFF OR
RASPBERRY FLUFF. A FAMILY FAVORITE.

$1/2$ cup cake meal

$1/4$ cup potato starch

$1/8$ teaspoon salt

8 extra-large eggs, separated

1 cup sugar

1 lemon, juice and rind

2 tablespoons orange juice

Preheat oven to 325°F.

Sift the dry ingredients and set aside.

Using an electric mixer, beat the egg yolks until thick. Add $1/2$ cup of the sugar, both juices, and rind. Continue beating until thick and fluffy. Fold in dry ingredients.

In a separate bowl, beat egg whites and a pinch of salt until foamy. Add the other $1/2$ cup of sugar gradually. Beat until stiff peaks form.

Fold egg yolk mixture into egg whites.

Pour into an ungreased 9- or 10-inch tube pan. Bake for 35 minutes. Turn oven up to 350°F until done. Test. Insert toothpick into cake; if it comes out clean, your cake is ready to remove from the oven.

Invert pan for several hours so cake can cool and stretch.

This cake may be frozen.

YIELD: 12 TO 14 SLICES

Passover Butter Cookies

❖ ❖ ❖

YOU WILL NOT BELIEVE THIS COOKIE. IT SIMPLY MELTS IN
YOUR MOUTH. FROM THE KITCHEN OF MY DEAR
FRIEND, BELLA.

Blend butter, sugar, vanilla, and salt until light and fluffy. Add yolks and blend well. Add chopped pecans. Add cake meal.

Form into balls, or drop from tip of teaspoon onto a cookie sheet lined with baking parchment. Depress in center and brush with lightly beaten egg whites.

Bake for 15 minutes, or until lightly browned.

Allow to cool on cookie sheet before removing.

YIELD: 7 TO 8 DOZEN

$^1/_2$ pound butter

$^3/_4$ cup sugar

1   teaspoon vanilla extract

$^1/_2$ teaspoon salt

2   eggs, separated

$1^1/_2$ cups chopped pecans

1   cup cake meal

Passover Lemon Filling

❖ ❖ ❖

THIS WAS AN OLD FAMILY FAVORITE THAT WAS SERVED OVER
THE TRADITIONAL SPONGE CAKE AND TOPPED WITH FRUIT.
THANK YOU, AUNTIE IDA.

1 3-ounce package lemon Jell-O	Combine Jell-O with boiling water. Set aside.
1/2 cup boiling water	Beat egg yolks until thick. Add the 3/4 cup of sugar. Beat again.
7 extra-large eggs, separated	Place in a double boiler. Add lemon juice and rind. Stir with a wooden spoon until thick. Remove from fire and add Jell-O at
3/4 cup plus 1/4 cup sugar	once. Blend well. Place over ice cubes to cool.
1/2 cup fresh lemon juice	Beat egg whites with the 1/4 cup of sugar until stiff. Add beaten
1 tablespoon grated fresh lemon rind	whites to cooled yolk mixture. Fold in carefully.

Pour into an attractive bowl. Cover with plastic wrap and store
in refrigerator until ready to serve.

YIELD: 12 TO 14 SERVINGS

Passover Raspberry Fluff

❖　❖　❖

THIS IS A FAVORITE FOR PASSOVER, OR ANY TIME OF THE
YEAR. SERVE OVER SPONGE CAKE OR A BROWNIE SQUARE
WITH A RASPBERRY SAUCE. YUMMY!

Place all ingredients in the large bowl of an electric mixer and
beat for about 20 minutes on #5 speed.

Pour into an attractive bowl for serving. Cover with plastic wrap
and place in freezer.

Remove from freezer 20 to 30 minutes before serving.

YIELD: 12 TO 14 SERVINGS

2　egg whites

1^1/$_3$ cups sugar

1　16-ounce bag
　unsweetened frozen
　berries

Passover Apple Cake

❖ ❖ ❖

THIS DISAPPEARS FAST! THE KIDS LOVE IT. I LOVE IT FOR BREAKFAST, WITH COFFEE.

3 eggs, separated

1 cup sugar

¹/₂ teaspoon salt

¹/₂ cup oil

¹/₂ cup (combination) lemon and orange juice

4 large apples (McIntosh or Granny Smith), coarsely chopped

grated rind of 1 lemon

grated rind of 1 orange

³/₄ cup cake meal

¹/₄ cup potato starch

TOPPING:

cinnamon and sugar and chopped pecans

Preheat oven to 375°F.

Beat egg whites until stiff and set aside.

In a large bowl, blend sugar, salt, egg yolks, oil, and juice. Add chopped apples and orange and lemon rind. Blend again. Add cake meal and potato starch.

Fold in beaten egg whites.

Pour batter into a greased pan approximately 7 × 11 inches.

Sprinkle with cinnamon and sugar and chopped pecans, or the following Streusel Topping.

Bake for 45 minutes. Cut into squares.

This freezes very well.

YIELD: 20 PIECES

Streusel Topping

❖　❖　❖

A NICE FINISH FOR THE FARFEL PUDDING OR THE
APPLE CAKE.

Blend ingredients until mealy. Sprinkle generously over the top of the farfel pudding or the apple cake, and bake according to instructions.

6 tablespoons margarine or butter

³/₄ cup cake meal

¹/₂ cup sugar

1 teaspoon cinnamon

Passover Cheesecake

❖   ❖   ❖

THIS IS A DENSE CHEESECAKE, LEMONY AND RICH. I HAVE
OFTEN SAID, I'VE NEVER MET A CHEESECAKE I DIDN'T LIKE.

4	*extra-large eggs*
1	*cup sugar*
$^1/_4$	*cup fresh lemon juice*
	grated rind of 1 lemon
$^1/_8$	*teaspoon salt*
1	*pound cottage cheese*
1	*pound cream cheese*
2	*cups sour cream*
$^1/_3$	*cup potato starch*

Preheat oven to 350°F.

Blend eggs, sugar, lemon juice, rind, and salt. Add cottage cheese, cream cheese, and sour cream and blend until smooth and creamy.

Add the potato starch and blend.

Pour into a well-greased 9-inch springform pan. Place in center of oven, with an oven liner on rack below to catch any leaking.

Bake for 60 to 70 minutes. Do not remove from oven. Do not open oven door. Allow cake to cool in oven for at least 4 hours.

Chill and serve with your favorite fruit sauce.

This cake can be frozen.

This can be adapted to a low-fat recipe by using nonfat cheeses and sour cream.

YIELD: 12 TO 16 SLICES

Passover Mousse Layer Cake

❖   ❖   ❖

MAHVELOUS, DARLINGS, JUST MAHVELOUS! THIS IS A
DELICIOUS WAY TO SERVE THE TRADITIONAL SPONGE CAKE.
THANK YOU, CARYN SMITH.

PREPARE A 10-EGG PASSOVER SPONGE CAKE (RECIPE IN THIS
SECTION) OR YOU MAY USE A MIX. USE A 10-INCH
SPRINGFORM PAN, UNGREASED. BAKE ACCORDING TO
INSTRUCTIONS. INVERT AND COOL. FREEZE.

Melt chocolate chips in water. Combine the sugar, vanilla, and egg yolks. Mix well. Add the chocolate to the yolk mixture and blend well.

In a separate bowl, beat egg whites until stiff. Fold into the chocolate mixture.

Slice frozen cake into 4 to 6 very thin layers. Place a layer of cake in the 10-inch springform and cover with the mousse. Alternate cake and mousse layers. Use all the crumbs; the layers do not have to be neat. End with a top layer of chocolate mousse.

Refrigerate for several hours or overnight.

When ready to serve, whip the cream with the 2 tablespoons sugar. Using a knife, loosen cake from sides of pan and place on a serving plate. Frost with the whipped cream. Sprinkle top with chocolate shavings.

YIELD: 16 TO 18 SERVINGS

MOUSSE:

1   12-ounce package semisweet chocolate chips

$1/4$ cup water

$1/4$ cup sugar

1   teaspoon vanilla extract

6   eggs (room temperature), separated

FROSTING:

$1/2$ pint heavy whipping cream

2   tablespoons sugar

chocolate shavings for top of cake

Fried Matzo Farfel

❖   ❖   ❖

WHEN MY GRANDCHILDREN WERE WITH ME FOR PASSOVER,
THIS WAS ALWAYS THEIR MAJOR REQUEST. I OFTEN MADE A
LARGE BATCH AHEAD OF TIME, AND FROZE IT. IT HEATS UP
WELL IN THE MICROWAVE.

2 cups matzo farfel	Soak the farfel in the hot water, and squeeze out as much as possible.
³/₄ cup hot water	
4 eggs, well beaten, or 1 cup egg substitute	Combine the farfel with the eggs, salt, spices, and rind.
1 teaspoon salt	
¹/₈ teaspoon ground cloves	Grease a large skillet with a vegetable spray. This will prevent sticking. Add about 3 tablespoons Nyafat or peanut oil. You may need more.
¹/₂ teaspoon ground cinnamon	
¹/₂ teaspoon grated orange rind	Heat well. Add farfel mixture. As it starts to fry, break up mixture with a large mixing spoon and keep turning until it is golden brown and slightly crispy. It should resemble browned scrambled eggs.
Nyafat or peanut oil for frying	
cinnamon and sugar	Remove from heat and serve with cinnamon and sugar.

YIELD: 6 SERVINGS

Passover Meat Loaf

❖　❖　❖

THIS IS DELICIOUS. WHY WAIT FOR PASSOVER? FROM THE
KITCHEN OF A DEAR LADY, NELL PEKARSKY.

Preheat oven to 350°F.

Combine the ground meat, onion, farfel, salt, pepper, water,
eggs, and $^1/_2$ cup of the tomato-mushroom sauce. Blend well.

Grease a baking dish. Shape the meat into a loaf (or use a loaf
pan).

Combine remaining tomato sauce, lemon juice, and sugar. Pour
over the meat loaf.

Bake for 1 hour. Baste several times while baking.

YIELD: 4 TO 6 SERVINGS

2　pounds ground meat

1　medium onion

1　cup crushed matzo
　　farfel

$^3/_4$　teaspoon salt

$^1/_8$　teaspoon pepper

$^1/_2$　cup water

2　eggs, well beaten

1　can tomato mush-
　　room sauce (avail-
　　able in the kosher
　　foods section of your
　　local supermarket)

$^1/_4$　cup fresh lemon juice

$^1/_2$　cup sugar

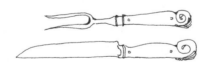

Passover Dairy Farfel Pudding

❖ ❖ ❖

**THIS IS A WONDERFUL DEPARTURE FROM THE HEAVY KUGELS.
TRY IT, YOU'LL LIKE IT.**

2¹/₂ cups matzo farfel

1   cup hot water

3   eggs, or ³/₄ cup egg substitute

¹/₄ cup sugar (or 1 teaspoon Sweet 'n Low)

2   cups cream-style cottage cheese (fat-free, optional)

1   cup sour cream (fat-free, optional)

5   tablespoons margarine or butter, melted

1   cup raisins

1   cup orange or apricot preserves (sugarfree, optional)

3   apples, coarsely chopped in food processor

1   teaspoon salt

1   teaspoon cinnamon

Preheat oven to 350°F.

Soak the farfel in the hot water and squeeze out excess liquid. Set aside.

Beat eggs until light. Add sugar and process until fluffy. Add cottage cheese, sour cream, margarine or butter, raisins, preserves, apples, salt, and cinnamon to egg mixture. Add the farfel and blend well.

Pour into a greased ovenproof serving dish, about 9 × 13 inches. Mix the nuts, sugar, and cinnamon together and sprinkle over the farfel mixture, or use Streusel Topping. (see page 251).

Bake for 60 to 70 minutes. This may be served hot or cold.

YIELD: 12 SERVINGS

TOPPING:

¹/₂ cup finely chopped walnuts or pecans

2   tablespoons sugar (or ¹/₄ teaspoon Sweet 'n Low)

1   teaspoon ground cinnamon

Passover Baked Chicken Breasts à l'Orange

❖   ❖   ❖

THIS IS JUST ONE OF THE MANY DISHES YOU CAN MAKE
FOR PASSOVER.

Preheat oven to 350°F.

In a plastic bag, mix cake meal with your favorite seasonings.

Place dampened chicken breasts in bag of cake meal and shake until lightly coated. Place chicken breasts in a well-greased baking dish and brush lightly with olive oil.

Cover tightly with foil and bake for 20 minutes.

Combine all the ingredients for the sauce.

Remove chicken from oven and brush generously with the sauce. Add a little water to the pan.

Return to oven, uncovered, and bake an additional 25 minutes, basting occasionally. Chicken should be well glazed.

If you prefer chicken parts with the bone in, or a capon, cut up, proceed according to instructions, and bake, covered, for 40 minutes. Remove from oven and brush generously with the sauce. Add a little water to the pan.

Return to oven, uncovered, and bake an additional 35 minutes, basting occasionally. Again, the parts should be well glazed.

YIELD: 6 TO 8 SERVINGS

8 to 10 skinless, boneless chicken breasts

cake meal

olive oil

SAUCE:

1   10- to 12-ounce jar sweet-and-sour sauce

1   tablespoon frozen orange juice concentrate

1   10-ounce jar sugar-free orange marmalade

1/4   cup white wine

1/4   cup ketchup

1/2   teaspoon dry mustard (dissolved in a little water)

Index

V

Veal chops, broiled or grilled,
124
Vegetables, 141–153
artichoke dip, 21
asparagus, oven-roasted, 150
cabbage, sweet-and-sour,
145
carrots, 143–144
eggplant relish, 152
marinade for, 60, 79, 153
Mexicali mold, 19
mushroom squares, 18
potato, 146–148
soups, 48, 50–54
spinach, 23, 133, 135
sweet potatoes, candied, 149
tomatoes, baked, 151
See also Salads

Velvet noodle pudding, 38
Vinegar, using to sour milk, 7

W

Whipped cream frosting, chocolate,
225
White
delite cake, 213
Persian caps, 176

Y

Yogurt cardamom dressing, 80
Yom Kippur, 9

Z

Zucchini-carrot soup, 51